D1590066

THE ESCAPE OF THE
Scharnhorst and Gneisenau

SEA BATTLES IN CLOSE-UP · 13

THE ESCAPE OF THE
Scharnhorst and Gneisenau

PETER KEMP

Naval Institute Press

First published 1975

Library of Congress Catalog Card No. 74-31679

ISBN 0-87021-819-0

Published and distributed in the United States
of America by the Naval Institute Press
Annapolis, Maryland, 21402

Printed in Great Britain

Contents

Acknowledgements

I owe a debt of gratitude to Rear Admiral Peter Buckley, Head of the Naval Historical Branch of the Ministry of Defence, to Mr Lawson, Curator of the German naval records, in the same Branch, and to Miss Riley, of the Naval Historical Branch Library, for their ready help in locating and making available a great many records of the action against the German squadron during their passage of the English Channel in February 1942.

I am equally grateful to Dr Noble Frankland, Director of the Imperial War Museum, and to Mr D. P. Mayne, Head of the Photographic Library of the Museum, for their help and courtesy in the search for photographs.

Introduction

The *Scharnhorst* and *Gneisenau* had arrived at Brest, the great French naval base in the north-western corner of the Bay of Biscay, on March 22nd, 1941 after a somewhat inglorious career. They were joined there on June 1st, 1941 by the *Prinz Eugen,* after a shorter, though no less inglorious, career at sea.

The *Scharnhorst* and *Gneisenau* were battle-cruisers, both completed and commissioned in 1939 shortly before the outbreak of World War II. In accordance with the Anglo-German naval treaty, which required each country to disclose the displacement of new naval construction to the other, they had been declared as 26,000 tons standard displacement. In fact, as with all the naval surface ships built under the Hitler régime, the declared displacement was false and they were built with a standard displacement of 31,800 tons. They had a designed speed of $31\frac{1}{2}$ knots and were armed with nine 11in guns, twelve 5.9in, fourteen 4.1in, and 62 smaller anti-aircraft guns. Each carried four aircraft.

They were remarkably handsome ships with high flared bows; indeed to the naval eye they were beautiful ships. They were well commanded and well manned, and if in the view of the British they were unduly timid and self-effacing in their operations, this was due not so much to lack of enterprise on the part of their admirals and captains as to their adherence to the rigid orders issued by the naval high command. Nevertheless, there were undoubtedly occasions when men of other navies would all have turned a blind eye on their orders.

Their first operation in the war took place on November 21st, 1939. The modest task set them was to operate in company to the north of the Faeroes as though they were about to make a break-out into the Atlantic, then retire to the far north until it was safe for them to return to Germany. The objective was to disrupt the British sea patrols in the area. On their way they ran into the British armed merchant cruiser *Rawalpindi* which, with her seven 6in guns, was no match for these relative giants. The *Scharnhorst* sank her in fourteen minutes and herself received one hit. The *Rawalpindi's* enemy report, however, was heard and the nearest ship to her in the British patrol line, the 6in cruiser *Newcastle,* closed at full speed. She sighted and was sighted by the two battle-cruisers. Admiral Marschall, flying his flag in the *Gneisenau,* thereupon decided to abandon the operation, signalled the *Scharnhorst* to follow, and retired to the eastward at full speed, later turning to the north where, in high latitudes, he could expect to remain undiscovered until it was safe to return to Germany. If they had turned on the *Newcastle* they could have sunk her with as much ease as the *Scharnhorst* had done the *Rawalpindi.* They reached Wilhelmshafen safely on November 27th.

Their next operation was the Norwegian campaign of 1940. Commanded now by Admiral Lütjens, with his flag in the *Scharnhorst,* their task was to cover the main naval operations of the invasion. Very early on the morning of April 9th they were sighted by the old British battle-cruiser *Renown,* which turned to the attack, working up to her full speed of 29 knots. The *Scharnhorst* and *Gneisenau* ran to the north and were eventually lost to sight by the *Renown* in a snowstorm, but not before the *Gneisenau* had been hit three times, wrecking her forward turret and putting her main armament control out of action. They ran as far north as latitude 69 before they turned and reached the safety of their home waters on April 12th. Here again, had they turned and engaged the *Renown,* they could have sunk her with relative ease, and probably with no more damage than the *Gneisenau* had suffered in running away.

In June, as the Norwegian campaign was drawing to its close, they were again sent into the North Sea to operate against the British forces which were being evacuated from northern Norway. On May 7th they came across a small

8

convoy of two ships escorted by a trawler in the central North Sea and promptly sank it, only to be recalled to their primary duty of operating against the withdrawal convoys further north by a signal from the high command. There, on June 9th, they sighted the British aircraft carrier *Glorious* escorted by the destroyers *Ardent* and *Acasta*. All three were sunk, but the *Acasta,* closing the battle-cruisers at full speed, succeeded in getting off a salvo of torpedoes before she was sent to the bottom. One of them hit the *Scharnhorst* abreast her after turret, inflicting serious damage, and the two ships retired to Trondheim. Eleven days later, the *Gneisenau,* on her way home, was attacked by the British submarine *Clyde.* One torpedo hit her, causing a great deal of damage. Eventually both battle-cruisers reached Kiel where the repairs to each of them took six months to complete.

In December 1940 the two ships left for a break-out into the Atlantic, but off the Norwegian coast the *Gneisenau* was damaged in a moderate sea and they returned to Kiel. A month later, on January 23rd, 1941, they set off again for the Atlantic with the initial objective of creating a diversion to facilitate the return to Germany of the pocket battleship *Admiral Scheer,* which had been raiding in the Atlantic. On the 28th they were sighted by the cruiser *Naiad,* but escaped by running at high speed into the far north. A week later they were in the Atlantic in search of British convoys, and on February 8th sighted the smoke of convoy HX106, homeward bound from Halifax. As they closed they sighted, and were sighted by, HMS *Ramillies,* the convoy's anti-raider escort. She was an old battleship of World War I vintage, some ten knots slower than the *Scharnhorst* and *Gneisenau,* but at the sight of her Admiral Lutjens withdrew at high speed. His caution was rewarded a fortnight later when the two ships came across the remnants of a west-bound convoy which had dispersed. They sank five merchant ships totalling 25,784 tons. Some of the ships succeeded in getting off a raider report on their wireless before they were sunk, and Lutjens, realising that this would alert the Royal Navy to his presence in these waters, withdrew to a new area of operations.

He made off to the south-west to try his luck against the African trade. On March 8th convoy SL67, homeward bound from Sierra Leone, was sighted, but as the *Scharnhorst* and *Gneisenau* approached they sighted her anti-raider escort, HMS *Malaya,* a battleship of slightly more ancient vintage than the *Ramillies.* With their greatly superior speed they had no difficulty in getting away without an engagement, and made their way back into mid-Atlantic. Here fortune again smiled on them and on March 15th and 16th they sank sixteen unescorted merchant ships to a total of 82,000 tons. They then made for Brest, evaded the British Home Fleet which was out searching for them, and reached port on March 22nd. They were sighted there by British photo reconnaissance aircraft on March 28th.

The *Prinz Eugen,* a heavy cruiser, was completed in 1940. Like the *Scharnhorst* and *Gneisenau,* her displacement was greatly in excess of that declared by the German Admiralty under the terms of the naval treaty, being 15,700 tons as compared with a declared tonnage of 10,000. She had a designed speed of 32½ knots and was armed with eight 8in guns, twelve 4.1in, and twenty small anti-aircraft pieces.

Her first operational duty was an Atlantic raiding cruise with the battleship *Bismarck* in May 1941. The original German plan was for these two ships to break out into the Atlantic through the Denmark Strait and to be joined by the *Scharnhorst* and *Gneisenau* from Brest to form a squadron of sufficient power to overwhelm British convoys with their single battleship escort. They were then to form an Atlantic squadron based on the French Biscay ports, a plan which would impose an almost impossible task on the British Home Fleet to contain it. This initial plan had to be modified when the *Scharnhorst* arrived at Brest requiring a refit before undertaking any further operations, but this still left the *Gneisenau* available to join the other two. She, however, was severely damaged by a torpedo in Brest harbour on April 6th and had to be dry-docked, receiving further severe damage during a bombing raid on April 11th.

During the operations which ended with the sinking of the *Bismarck* by the Home Fleet on May 27th, 1941, the *Prinz*

Eugen had been detached by the *Bismarck* and ordered to proceed independently to a supply tanker in the north-west Atlantic, partly to act as a decoy and draw away the chasing British Home Fleet from the *Bismarck* so that she could make her escape undetected, and partly, after replenishment of fuel, to act independently against British Atlantic trade. Captain Brinkmann of the *Prinz Eugen,* however, had other views. He was unhappy at this abrupt division of the force and decided to make to the southward, where another replenishment tanker had been stationed. Here he completed with fuel, decided against his instructions to harry trade in the Atlantic, and instead made his way to Brest to join the *Scharnhorst* and *Gneisenau.* The *Prinz Eugen* arrived there on June 1st, and was photographed by British reconnaissance aircraft on the 4th.

The presence of these three ships in Brest presented a considerable problem to the British Admiralty and the Home Fleet. The most menacing aspect of their presence lay in the threat they posed to the large troop convoys carrying reinforcements to the Middle East, which now had not only to be routed much further out into the Atlantic as they made their way south to the Cape of Good Hope but also to be very heavily escorted with capital ships in case the German squadron from Brest should break out to attack them. To remove the threat, the Admiralty requested the Air Ministry to arrange as heavy a programme of bombing as possible in order to immobilise the ships.

The first to be damaged was the *Gneisenau.* As noticed above, she was hit by a torpedo from a torpedo-bomber as she lay at a buoy in the harbour. Her plating and wing bulkheads on the starboard side were destroyed over a length of some 30-40ft; one transverse bulkhead was punched out, her torpedo bulkhead was stove in and torn away from the armoured deck; the starboard turbine-room bulkhead and shaft tunnel were damaged and the shaft and main bearings twisted; the after anti-aircraft computer room was completely destroyed and the pedestal mounting of C turret was partially damaged. There was additional damage from flooding in two of her engine-rooms, and repairs were estimated to take four months. She was taken into dry-dock on the following day, but during the night raid on April 10th-11th she was again hit, this time by four bombs, one of them heavy. Two more exploded on the side of the dock. The casualties caused were serious, with 50 dead and over 90 wounded, and very considerable damage was incurred, made more severe in some cases by several fires which broke out after the bombing. These became so serious that respirators had to be issued to the ship's company. The first bomb to hit her stove in her deck armour and the second bomb fell through the hole made by the first, exploding alongside B turret. The third bomb penetrated the spar deck, upper deck and battery deck before exploding, and the fourth failed to explode. Her upper deck was badly torn by the bombs which burst on the side of the dock.

Soon after the damage from these two attacks had been repaired, but before she could carry out any trials, she was damaged again during an afternoon raid on December 18th, 1941. No bomb registered a direct hit, but several fell around the dock and exploded, causing blast damage. And finally she was severely damaged once more during an attack on January 6th, 1942 when a bomb fell and exploded between her hull and the side of the dock, tearing open her outer plating and causing several of her internal compartments to be flooded. Repairs from this last bombing were completed on January 25th.

The *Scharnhorst,* after her refit at Brest following her first arrival there, was ordered to La Pallice on July 21st, 1941 to carry out engine trials, gunnery and torpedo firing practice. This was, in part, an attempt by Admiral Raeder to discover whether an alternative base to Brest could be found beyond the range of British bombers. It was hoped eventually to persuade the French to agree to the use of a still more southerly port, possibly Bordeaux, for the German Atlantic squadron, but in the event that never materialised. The *Scharnhorst* was discovered at La Pallice on July 24th and attacked by a force of fifteen bombers which hit her five times. All her electrical installations were severely damaged, C turret was put out of action, and structural damage caused in her engine-rooms, fuel tanks, and starboard propellor shaft. One bomb went through her double bottoms and exploded, causing so much flooding that she had on board 3,000 tons of water and took on a list of six degrees. The estimated time for her repair was four months, and in fact she was out of action for the remainder of the year.

The *Prinz Eugen's* turn came on July 1st, 1941 when, during a night attack, a bomb hit her on the port side forward, penetrated the armoured deck, killing 51 of her ship's company and wounding 32. The gunnery transmitting station, compass compartment, switch room and amplifier compartment were wrecked and completely destroyed, and she was not ready for service until the beginning of 1942.

The congregation of capital ships in the Bay of Biscay had been one of the main planks in Admiral Raeder's grand strategy. He could readily appreciate its value to Germany as a powerful threat to British essential trade across the Atlantic and to the big troop and supply convoys by which the Middle East theatre of war was nourished. He knew, too, how great a thorn it would represent in the side of the British Home Fleet. With a powerful naval threat in northern Norway, represented by the battleship *Tirpitz* which he sent north to Trondheim on January 23rd, 1942, to tie down the Home Fleet at Scapa Flow, the Brest squadron should have had many chances of slipping out into the Atlantic to create havoc on the convoy routes. It was an astute move which held the British Home Fleet in a cleft stick.

It was a policy which was, in the end, brought to nought by the intransigence of Goering, on whom Raeder relied to provide adequate fighter protection against the inevitable air attacks which were bound to develop when the presence of the German ships was discovered by the British. Goering was able to persuade Hitler that the German Air Force had too many priority commitments in other war theatres to spare fighters for the defence of Brest. He was closer to the Führer than was Raeder, his influence was greater, and so the ships at Brest were required to provide their own defence.

This was the main reason for the abandonment of La Pallice as the operational base for the Atlantic squadron. It was all the more desirable as a base for, being considerably further from the bomber airfields of Britain than Brest and with fighter protection from the German Air Force, it would have served Raeder's purpose until an even more southerly base could be obtained from the French. But Brest was more easily defended if the ships had to provide their own anti-aircraft defence, and so Brest it had to be.

The dockyard at Brest was ringed with anti-aircraft batteries, to which the ships' own anti-aircraft armament added a substantial strength. Vast areas of camouflage netting were spread over the ships as they lay in dock or alongside the dockyard walls, and, late in 1941, artificial fog-making apparatus was installed to cover the dockyard area with a thick screen of smoke. The German Air Force, consulted on this last measure, condemned it as completely useless; nevertheless it did, when used, make the three targets invisible from the air and so undoubtedly made accurate bombing impossible. It also served a further, less tangible, purpose in arousing local opposition to the ceaseless British attacks. The all-enveloping smoke, combined with the great weight of anti-aircraft fire, made blind, or area, bombing the only possible method of attack, and the civilian town of Brest suffered just as heavily from British bombs as did the dockyard. It was a fact hardly likely to enhance any local French sympathy for the British cause.

Raeder's strategical plans miscarried, partly by the sinking of the *Bismarck* in May 1941 and partly through the operations of Bomber Command which kept the three big ships at Brest more or less permanently out of action. They came eventually to an end partly through Hitler's famous "intuition" and partly through Goering's intransigence.

Towards the end of 1941 Hitler convinced himself that Britain was planning an invasion of northern Norway. So strongly did he hold this view that he decided to concentrate the main naval force of Germany in those waters, and though Raeder argued strongly for his Atlantic strategy, Hitler was adamant. The *Tirpitz* was immediately available, of course, and was there by the beginning of 1942, but Hitler wanted more. It was at that stage that Goering again stepped into the picture, assuring Hitler again that the German Air Force had not sufficient strength to undertake responsibility for the defence of Brest. German ships, for lack of full fighter defence capability, were suffering damage, but he, Goering, could not help that. He had not sent them to Brest. These two forces combined — Hitler's belief in a British plan to invade Norway and Goering's declining of responsibility — resulted in an ultimatum to Raeder. Either he must bring the ships in Brest back to Germany or to Norway, or they must be dismantled at Brest and their guns and crews brought back to stiffen the Norwegian defence.

Dismantling, in Raeder's view, was the worse of the two alternatives, a confession of defeat which would not only severely depress public morale in Germany but equally enhance that in Britain and her allies. Reluctantly he agreed to the second alternative of bringing the ships home to Germany, and planning began actively in January 1942. The operational plan (see Part III) was left entirely in the hands of Vice-Admiral Ciliax, commanding the Atlantic squadron. Quite early in the planning it was decided that the English Channel route was preferable to that north of Scotland through the Iceland/Faroes gap, and this was accepted at a conference at Hitler's headquarters on January 12th, 1942 at which both the Naval and Air Staffs were present. According to the naval version of this conference, "he (Hitler) compared the situation of the Brest group with that of a patient having cancer, who was doomed unless he submitted to an operation. An operation, on the other hand, even though it might have to be a drastic one, would offer at least some hope that the patient's life might be saved. The passage of the German ships through the Channel would be such an operation and had therefore to be attempted."

It was fortunate for Vice-Admiral Ciliax that the damage to the *Gneisenau* during the air raid on January 6th, 1942, though serious, was fairly quickly repairable. She was able to carry out engine trials and gunnery practice in Brest roads on January 27th. After January 6th there were no hits on any of the three big ships and all of them were ready for sea by the end of the month although the lack of opportunities for trials and training gave some cause for apprehension as to the fighting efficiency of their crews.

At the end of January Vice-Admiral Ciliax was ordered to report to Hitler's headquarters where his plan was discussed in detail and where Hitler gave him his personal permission to go ahead. Ciliax appeared to fare better with his Führer than had Raeder. "It was on this occasion", he wrote, "that I noticed (contrary to allegations) that Hitler showed himself quite amenable to rational suggestions and arguments in spite of the fact that in details his opinion differed from my own. In the end my plan was accepted unaltered".

As the days of February opened, the first preliminary moves in the German operational plan were made. A considerable increase in minesweeping routines built up in the English Channel and along the Belgian and Dutch coasts. Destroyers steamed westward down the Channel and into the port of Brest. Tugs were stationed in French, Belgian and Dutch harbours to stand by in case of emergency.

The movement of the destroyers to Brest did not go unnoticed in Britain, though most of the minesweeping did, as it was all done during the hours of darkness. By February 3rd the Admiralty were convinced that some move of the Brest squadron was imminent and issued their appreciation of the situation to naval and air force commands. By February 8th Air Marshal Sir Philip Joubert, commanding Coastal Command, also issued an appreciation, forecasting that the German ships might leave Brest and make their way up Channel on any day after February 10th. In the event, they began their break-out on the 11th.

CHAPTER ONE

The British Planning

When the two German battle-cruisers were first located at Brest by photographic reconnaissance on March 28th, 1941, plans were drawn up within a month to deal with them in the event of a quick break-back to Germany. It was agreed between the Admiralty and the Air Ministry that any operation to try to stop them must be basically an air operation in view of the current commitments of the British Home Fleet, though the Admiralty did undertake to play a part in the operation to the utmost of their ability, which was envisaged as light surface forces from Dover.

The Home Fleet's main commitments at this time, and throughout the remainder of 1941 and indeed into 1942, were twofold and neither could be in any way relaxed. One of them was to cover any German break-out by surface ships into the Atlantic with its consequent threat to the convoy supply routes from Canada and the USA. It was known in the British Admiralty that the *Bismarck* and the heavy cruiser *Prinz Eugen* were ready for operations, and that the *Bismarck's* sister ship, *Tirpitz,* would be completed and worked up during 1941. The dependence of Britain on the Atlantic convoy routes, if she were to remain a viable fighting force, was absolute, and the prospect of a fast and powerful German battleship squadron loose on the convoy routes, particularly with two battle-cruisers similarly poised in Brest and available as local reinforcement, was unthinkable. A sufficiently powerful Home Fleet had to be held in Scapa Flow to stop any such attempt by the German navy.

The other supreme Home Fleet commitment was the series of WS convoys to the Middle East. These were large troop convoys, frequently carrying from 70,000-80,000 men, destined as reinforcements for the 8th Army in Egypt. With two enemy battle-cruisers now in Brest they not only had to be routed much farther out into the Atlantic, considerably increasing their passage time, but also required battleship escort in case the *Scharnhorst* and/or *Gneisenau* came out to attack them. These WS convoys were an operational requirement on the grand strategy scale that took an absolute priority. There was no question of cancelling them, or of reducing their frequency, to free a capital ship for a possible operation of which the date, and indeed the event, was entirely problematic. It would make a complete strategic nonsense to do so.

This was as fully realised in the Air Ministry as in the Admiralty, and on April 29th, 1941, the Air Ministry issued its operational directive to the three commands, Coastal, Bomber and Fighter. In view of the subsequent events when the battle-cruisers and the *Prinz Eugen* made their break through the Channel on February 11th-12th, 1942, two clauses of this directive can perhaps be quoted:

5 Light surface forces will deliver torpedo attacks against these vessels during their passage of the Straits (of Dover).

7 It is considered unlikely that the enemy would attempt the passage of the Straits in daylight. If however this should be attempted a unique opportunity will be offered to both our surface vessels and air striking forces to engage the enemy ships in force whilst in the Straits of Dover. Such attacks are to be delivered to the maximum practicable effort under fighter cover to be provided by the Air Officer Commanding-in-Chief Fighter Command. The Admiralty are arranging that in these circumstances the VA Dover (Vice-Admiral Bertram W. Ramsay) will keep 11 Group (Fighter Command) and 16 Group (Coastal Command) informed of attacks carried out by surface vessels in order that air attacks may be co-ordinated therewith and fighter cover provided.

The Air Ministry directive gave the code-word *Fuller* to the operation and declared that it would be brought immediately into action with the order "Executive Fuller"

No more would be required to get all forces engaged on the move.

In due course the three air force commands issued their operational orders for *Fuller*. That for Fighter Command was dated October 5th, 1941, and in view of subsequent controversy, one order may be quoted:

"R/T and 'Pipsqueak' silence is to be maintained on the outward journey, except in emergency, until such time as the enemy has been engaged".

It was signed by the Senior Air Staff Officer at Fighter Command, Group Captain Beamish.

The *Prinz Eugen* was first photographed at Brest on June 4th, 1941, having arrived there three days earlier after her unsuccessful foray into the Atlantic with the *Bismarck*. The three ships were kept under frequent observation throughout the rest of the year, and although there was no knowledge in Britain of the full extent of the damage caused by the bombing raids, it was at least known that they had been hit and that some damage had been caused. Information to this end came from French dockyard workers attached to British Intelligence as agents, one of whom worked on the day shift and the other on the night shift. A French naval officer in Brest was also serving as an agent and his reports were highly graded. With this valuable information, added to that deduced from air photographs, a reasonably accurate picture of the state of affairs in Brest in relation to the condition of the enemy ships was maintained in Britain.

As reports of damage and delays filtered through, the immediate urgency of Operation *Fuller* faded. It was not until near the end of January 1942 that the first signs of a forthcoming movement became apparent. They came first from the agents in Brest, who reported all three ships as operational and signs of extra activity in the dockyard. A day or two later an appreciation of their probable course of action was received from the French naval officer, who gave it as his opinion that the three ships would leave Brest in darkness and would force their way through the Straits of Dover in daylight. It is now known, of course, that his opinion was absolutely correct, but at that time it conflicted with the widely-held view in Britain that the German ships would try to ensure the benefit of darkness to help them through the most dangerous stretch of their passage. But in any case it was hoped that one of the two dockyard workers would get the essential message through when it was seen that the ships were about to move. In the event it was unfortunate that messages from one of them — the one whose hours of work might have enabled him to get off a signal that the ships had sailed — ceased three days before the squadron left Brest. It was thought at the time that he had fallen into the hands of German counter-espionage agents.

When, at the end of January, signs were beginning to accumulate that some operation from Brest was about to take place, the Admiralty considered anew the possible movements which the three ships might make. They had, from the earliest days, considered that a return to Germany through the English Channel was their most likely course of action, an opinion which the Air Ministry shared, as evidenced by the directive issued to the three air commands. But it was thought wiser at this stage to review all the options open to the Germans and to re-assess them to find the most likely.

It was thought that there were four possible courses of action which they could take:

1 To make their way to an Italian base, possibly Genoa, where they could work up to full operational efficiency without interruption from frequent bombing raids.
2 To operate against the convoy routes in the Atlantic.
3 To return to Germany, or Norway, by way of the Denmark Strait or the Iceland-Faroes gap.
4 To return to Germany by way of the English Channel.

The only way to an Italian port was through the Straits of Gibraltar, which would mean running the gauntlet of Force H, based at Gibraltar. It was thought unlikely that these ships, which had as yet had no chance of working up to operational efficiency, would risk such a course. The same reasoning was held to make the second course of action equally unlikely, for crews not yet trained to full efficiency would certainly prejudice the success of prolonged

20

operations of this nature. The ships, too, had not been worked up and required many more hours and days of engine trials, weapon training etc, before they could be considered efficient, another powerful argument against such a course.

These arguments left only the return to Germany or Norway, by way of northern waters or the English Channel, as the only two alternatives left. Both had their attractions and both their objections. In favour of the northern passage was the fact that it had been, and still was, used successfully by German ships without interception by British forces. The nights in the northern waters were very long and very dark. Nevertheless, there were also objections. The British Home Fleet was based at Scapa Flow, and carrier-borne aircraft could search a very wide area of sea. And perhaps more important, the whole long passage would have to be made without benefit of German air cover. In favour of the Channel route was its shortness — some 550 miles compared with some thousands; the fact that all the passage during daylight would be made under massive fighter cover, and that the whole of the passage, from Brest to Brunsbuttel, would be made with a destroyer and torpedo-boat screen augmented during light hours with a strong E-boat escort. Against it was the fact that it would be made close to the English coast and in easy range of very heavy air attack. The German command was as well aware as the British that they need not fear attack in these narrow waters by capital ships; they could assess the strategic situation with just as much realism as the Admiralty. And while they fully expected attack by destroyers and motor torpedo boats, they would have with them a sufficient strength of destroyers and E-boats to force the attackers to fire their torpedoes at long range.

It was this reasoning which decided the Admiralty to accept the Channel passage as the most likely course of action to be adopted. They issued an appreciation on February 2nd. "The Brest ships", it ran, "cannot be fully efficient yet; although they have led a charmed life the Germans must be anxious to get them away to a safer harbour. Only if we can anticipate the plan of their

21

departure can our chances of destroying them be good.

"There are three, possibly five, large and five small destroyers at Brest, all of which have recently arrived. Minesweeping operations in the approaches to Brest have recently been seen. There has been no distinctive shape detected in any of the air reconnaissances flown by the Germans in the vicinity of Brest. There are indications of movement but no indication of its direction.

"The short cut for the German ships is via the English Channel. It is 240 miles from Brest to Cherbourg and another 120 miles from Cherbourg to the Dover Straits. Whilst ships could make the passage from Brest to Cherbourg or from Cherbourg to the Dover Straits, in the same dark period, they could not make the complete passage from Brest to the Dover Straits in one dark period.

"At first sight this passage up the Channel seems hazardous for the Germans. It is probable, however, that as their heavy ships are not fully efficient, they could prefer such a passage, relying for their security on the destroyers and aircraft, which are efficient, and knowing full well that we have no heavy ships to oppose them in the Channel.

"We might well therefore find the two battle-cruisers and the heavy 8in cruiser with five large and five small destroyers, also say, twenty fighters constantly overhead (with reinforcements within call) proceeding up the Channel. To meet this sortie we have about six MTBs at Dover, but no destroyers with torpedo armament.

"Our bombers have shown that we cannot place much reliance on them to damage the enemy, whilst our Coastal Command torpedo-bomber aircraft will not muster more than nine.

"Taking all factors into consideration, it appears that the German ships can pass east up the Channel with much less risk than they will incur if they attempt an ocean passage".

This Admiralty appreciation was followed six days later by one from the Commander-in-Chief of Coastal Command, Sir Philip Joubert:

"There are four large destroyers and a number of smaller torpedo boats and mine-sweepers in Brest. There are indications that the number of destroyers may be increased.

During the past few days all three big ships have been carrying out exercises in open waters and should be reasonably ready for sea.

"As from the 10th the weather conditions in the Channel would be reasonable for an attempted break-through in darkness. On February 15th there will be no moon and the tidal conditions at Dover would favour a passage between 04.00 hrs and 06.00 hrs.

"Finally, the large number of destroyers and small torpedo boats that have been concentrated at Brest would seem to indicate an attempt to force a way up the Channel — any time after Tuesday, February 10th".

The Admiralty, Air Ministry, the three air commands, and the naval headquarters at Dover were unanimous in expecting the German squadron to try to force the narrowest part of their passage, the Straits of Dover, during the hours of darkness. It was appreciated that they would select a period of little or no moon, and a day when they could expect the maximum help from the tide during their passage. In mid-February there were approximately fourteen hours of darkness to ten of daylight, and the new moon was on the 15th, bringing with it spring tides. It was considered that the Germans would most probably aim to make the passage of the Dover Straits at or near high water to minimise any danger from mines and at a time at or shortly before sunrise so that they had the maximum period of darkness during the passage from Brest up Channel. Sunrise on February 12th was at 08.25 hrs and high water at Dover at 09.20 hrs. It appeared therefore that February 12th was quite a likely day for the operation, even though it was recognised that such a timetable would mean that the German ships would have to leave Brest during hours of daylight.

The only naval forces at Dover were motor torpedo boats and motor gunboats, and when the Admiralty issued its appreciation to the effect that the passage of the English Channel was the most likely course to be adopted by the Germans, steps were taken to reinforce the available naval force to the utmost possible. The Commander-in-Chief at the Nore was asked to arrange for six destroyers, with torpedo armament, and six motor torpedo boats to be placed under the operational control of the Vice-Admiral, Dover. As Dover was an unsuitable harbour for destroyers, they were to operate from Harwich, and the motor torpedo boats would operate from their own base at Ramsgate. In the event these six motor torpedo boats were reduced to three following an attack on German destroyers off Gravelines in the Channel on the night of February 8th-9th when, on their return, MTBs 30, 31 and 34 ran ashore off the South Foreland and were so badly damaged that they were unfit for further service. It was doubly unfortunate as these three were of the latest type with the best performance.

In addition to these reinforcements from the Nore Command, the Commander-in-Chief at Plymouth was ordered to sail the fast minelayer, HMS *Welshman,* complete with mines, to Portsmouth where she would come under the operational orders of the Vice-Admiral, Dover. He was also ordered to operate the similar minelayer, HMS *Manxman,* as he thought best with the object of laying minefields in the expected path of the German squadron. HMS *Plover,* another fast minelayer, had already laid a series of minefields north of Dunkirk between January 15th and 23rd, and it was hoped that some of these fields were still undiscovered by the enemy.

It was Vice-Admiral Ramsay, at Dover, after a review of his slender forces, who suggested that they be augmented by six Swordfish torpedo bombers of No 825 Squadron, to be stationed at the RAF airfield at Manston. The torpedo-bombing role of the combined attack was, in fact, purely a Royal Air Force commitment with the Beauforts of Coastal Command, but Admiral Ramsay was not entirely convinced of their ability to hit fast-moving warships and so asked for the Swordfish as an additional attacking force. The Admiralty concurred with his request and the Swordfish were ordered to Manston from Lee-on-Solent, arriving there on February 4th.

The Vice-Admiral, Dover's plan was to launch a combined sea and air torpedo attack with the Dover motor torpedo boats and Swordfish aircraft in the Straits of Dover, either off Calais or Cap Blanc Nez according to the degree or prior warning received, with the intention of stopping or slowing down the enemy in an area where not only would the shore batteries be within range but also where radar could pinpoint the enemy for ranging purposes. The motor torpedo boats from Ramsgate were to engage the enemy between the Sandettié and Outer Ruytingen Banks, some 21 miles south-east of Ramsgate, where there was a chance of forcing the enemy to turn away on to one of HMS *Plover's* previously laid minefields. This was to be followed by a torpedo attack from the destroyers in a position approximately 30 miles to the north-east of the West Hinder Bank, in waters where the destroyers could move freely in relation to our own minefields and well beyond range of German coastal gun batteries. It was hoped that, during their passage through the Straits, one or more of the enemy ships would have been damaged by torpedo or mine to make easier the task of the destroyers.

In the event of the German battle-cruisers traversing the Straits during a period of moonlight, the Swordfish were to attack in squadron formation; if they chose a dark period the Swordfish were to attack singly. They were to be directed onto the target by the Royal Air Force controller at Swingate, the site of one of the small coastal radar stations, and arrangements were made for Hurricane fighters to illuminate the German squadron with flares. Positions, course and speed of the enemy would be broadcast every five minutes from the radar plot so that all forces engaged could very quickly work out their interception courses. Finally, the commanding officers of all forces to be engaged were fully briefed, not only in their own tasks but also in those of the other forces, and instructions were given that the whole operation would be put in train by the signal "Proceed in execution of previous orders". No further signal was required to send them all on their way.

On the assumption that the most likely time of arrival of the German ships in the Dover Straits was at or just before dawn, all the naval forces were to be at immediate notice from 04.00 hrs every morning until a time based on the time of high water at Dover. On February 12th, this time was 07.00 hrs. From this time onwards the naval forces reverted to four hours' notice, so that they could make such arrangements for normal maintenance routines as they might require. If, by chance, the German ships were to make a daylight passage instead of a night passage, the daily fighter reconnaissance flights over the Channel, combined with the Coastal Command night patrols in the western Channel, were designed to give plenty of time to bring all forces to immediate notice and get them on the move.

The Royal Air Force had a more complex business in producing an integrated plan of attack, partly because there was no one officer or command made responsible for planning the operation as a whole, and partly because the three commands involved, Coastal, Bomber and Fighter, were virtually autonomous within their own spheres. Integrated planning, too, was made more difficult by the very high degree of secrecy which was maintained around Operation *Fuller*. Only the most senior officers in each command were allowed to know what *Fuller* meant, and the speed with which the reality materialised on the morning of February 12th resulted in a majority of pilots and aircrews being ordered to fly off with no knowledge of what it was they were to look for and attack. The failure to concentrate the forces detailed for the attack, particularly in the case of Coastal Command (see Chapter 3), also led to a sad dissipation of attacking force. The most hopeful single weapon of attack was the Beaufort torpedo-bombers of Coastal Command, and the overall air plan called for a concentrated attack by the three available squadrons under a heavy fighter cover. In the event, partly because of the lack of previous concentration and partly because of a failure to ensure that aircraft torpedoes were in the same place as the aircraft, the co-ordinated attack by three squadrons developed into a series of unco-ordinated attacks by aircraft in ones and twos, spread out over three hours in steadily worsening weather conditions. The other commitment to fall to Coastal Command within the overall air plan was the requirement to fly nightly reconnaissance patrols throughout the hours of darkness in the western and central Channel. Three patrols were laid down, a westerly one, known as "Stopper", off the entrance to Brest, a central patrol, known as "Line SE",

26

between Ushant and the Île de Bréhat, and an eastern one, known as "Habo", between Le Havre and Boulogne. These three were to be flown by Hudson aircraft fitted with ASV (radar) sets and were to be continuous from dusk to dawn. It was on these three patrols, and daylight ones flown by Fighter Command (see Chapter 3) that reliance was placed for an early warning of the German sortie.

For the attack by bombers, a total of 300 aircraft had been set aside for the task of making an attack, in the words of the initial Air Ministry directive, "to the maximum practical effort". This number was allocated to Operation *Fuller* on February 4th, 1942, and they were held at two hours' notice. This meant, of course, that these aircraft were unable to take part in the night bombing attacks on Germany, and the Commander-in-Chief of Bomber Command made a request to the Air Ministry on February 7th for their release from *Fuller* so that they could participate in the night attacks which, in the view of Bomber Command, should take priority over any problematical operation in the Channel. The Air Ministry consulted the Admiralty on February 8th, but were told that, in the naval view, the break-out of the German ships was imminent and that, in the overall view, their destruction was probably more desirable and more likely to affect the whole course of the war than the raids on Germany. The Admiralty assessment was passed to Bomber Command by the Air Ministry, but the Commander-in-Chief unilaterally decided to withdraw 200 of the 300 bombers from their *Fuller* commitment and to place the remainder on normal stand-by notice. It was perhaps unfortunate, in view of the overall air plan, that neither the Air Ministry nor the other commands, Coastal and Fighter, were informed of this decision. In the event, when the *Scharnhorst, Gneisenau,* and *Prinz Eugen* were reported in the Channel in the late morning of February 12th, the main force of bombers was not airborne for three hours after the receipt of the information, and thus had to make their attacks in the late afternoon when the light was going and the conditions for bombing were at their worst. It is even conceivable, had they managed to be airborne an hour earlier, that they would have found the *Scharnhorst* stopped after hitting her first mine at 14.31 hrs.

The Fighter Command part of the total air plan was one of co-operation with the other two commands and with the naval headquarters at Dover. This co-operation was to be arranged by direct telephone with 11 Group headquarters and fighter cover to be allocated as necessary by 11 Group Controller. In addition, it was a Fighter Command commitment to maintain two-hourly daylight patrols between Fécamp and Ostend, known as the "Jim Crow" patrols, and in the event it was one of these which first sighted the German squadron.

The mining programme was co-ordinated by Vice-Admiral Ramsay. Towards the end of January requests were made by him to the Air Ministry for aircraft of Bomber Command to lay five fields of magnetic mines off the Frisian Islands along the possible route of the Brest squadron after entering German waters. These five fields escaped the attention of the German minesweepers and it was in fact these mines which were responsible for the only damage inflicted on the two battle-cruisers during their passage, the *Scharnhorst* exploding two and the *Gneisenau* one. HMS *Plover,* operating from the Nore, laid three minefields in the last week in January to the north-eastward of the Dover Straits, one between the West Hinder and Dyck Banks and two north-east of the Outer Ruytingen Bank. The most southerly of these was discovered by the Germans a day or two after it had been laid, when the destroyer *Bruno Heinemann,* on the way to Brest to form part of the close escort, exploded one of them and was sunk (see Chapter 2). As a result the planned route of the battle-cruisers was altered to pass to the northward of the area, which took them clear of the second minefield but brought them over the field between the West Hinder and Dyck Banks. By chance the ships must have passed between the mines and not directly over them.

A third series of four minefields was laid by HMS *Welshman* on the night of February 7th-8th to the north of Cape Barfleur, off Cap d'Antifer and St Valery, and west of Etaples. The first was discovered on the night of February

10th-11th when one of the German minesweepers, *M1208,* exploded one of the mines and sank, thus providing information in time for the planned route of the German squadron to be altered to allow it to pass harmlessly to the southward of the field. The mines off Etaples were discovered by the German 1st Minesweeping Flotilla on the night of February 11th-12th while the German squadron was in fact on its way up the Channel. The sweeping of a narrow channel through it was only just completed by the time the *Scharnhorst, Gneisenau* and *Prinz Eugen* arrived, and they were forced to reduce speed to ten knots as they went through. The other two minefields were just off the route planned by Vice-Admiral Ciliax and so did not affect the passage of the ships.

One other aspect of British planning, though independent of Air Ministry, Admiralty, and VA, Dover, was the action taken by the Flag Officer Submarines, Vice-Admiral Sir Max Horton, in sending the modern submarine *Sealion* to a patrol area in the approaches to Brest in the hope of being able to torpedo one of the German ships while they were exercising off the port in preparation for their break-out. Because of very heavy losses in the Mediterranean during recent months, and replacements sent there to fill the gaps, there were no other modern submarines available to strengthen this particular patrol, though two of the older World War I H-boats had been allocated patrol areas in the Bay of Biscay. They were, however, unsuitable for work in inshore waters. The *Sealion's* orders were to patrol the Brest approaches during daylight hours, attacking if the chance offered. Each night she had, of course, to withdraw to seaward to recharge her batteries for the following day's patrol.

CHAPTER TWO

The German Planning

The German planning for the break-out from Brest of the *Scharnhorst, Gneisenau* and *Prinz Eugen* was, as ever with German naval planning, detailed and meticulous. It sprang basically from Hitler's decision in December, 1941, to reinforce the naval squadrons in northern Norway with the ships from Brest, a decision taken in his firm conviction that an invasion of northern Norway was being planned by the British.

There were other reasons for contemplating such a move, and they were all listed by Vice-Admiral Ciliax, commanding the Brest squadron, in his own account of the operation. These were, in his words:

1 It was realised that operations in the Atlantic were not likely to be successful because of the lack of bases there and the uncertainty of supplying naval forces by means of store-ships. The latter would have to run added risks in view of the tightening-up of British defensive measures, no German aircraft-carrier being available.

2 Remaining in the Bay of Biscay for the purpose of tying down British naval forces and limited advances to the west without the possibility of refuelling exposed our vessels in port to aerial attack and consequently continuous risk of damage.

3 The reinforcement of the Norwegian stronghold would reduce the threat of invasion from the east (? west) and simultaneously would increase the opportunities for attacks on convoy routes to the Russian Arctic ports.

Admiral Ciliax also made a note of the disadvantages to Germany of a withdrawal of the squadron from Brest.

These, in his opinion, were:

1 On the other hand the relinquishing of what was, after all, the first German naval station for larger units of the Fleet in ports along the open Atlantic coast would be severely felt.
2 One had to accept the fact that the withdrawal of battleships from the Atlantic coast where their presence necessarily constituted a potential threat would cause the British Admiralty considerable pleasure.

For two or three weeks after Hitler's first announcement that the three ships in Brest were to go to Norway, the German naval staff, in the person of Admiral Raeder, fought a rearguard action to get the decision reversed. Raeder, whose understanding of the strategic values of warships was unequalled in Germany, could well understand the embarrassing problems which the presence of a German heavy squadron in Brest cast on the shoulders of the Admiralty in London and the Home Fleet in Scapa Flow, and he was reluctant to surrender this great advantage. But two factors in the situation made all his arguments fail. One was the success of the Royal Air Force in their bombing raids on the ships at Brest, which for nearly nine months had kept all three ships virtually out of action; the other was the success of Goering in convincing Hitler that the German Air Force had greater operational priorities than the provision of an adequate fighter force to keep the RAF bombers at bay. Faced with this insoluble problem Raeder had to agree to the withdrawal.

Active planning for the sortie began on January 12th, 1942, when Hitler laid down his alternatives of dismantling the ships at Brest or of bringing them home. Vice-Admiral Ciliax who was to command the force at sea, had at first an open mind as to which of the two possible routes home to select. "As regards the transfer to the east", he wrote, "there were two possibilities, either via the Atlantic and north of the British Isles, or via the Channel. There seemed at first to be nothing against either of these plans". The German naval staff expressed a preference for the northern route, but Vice-Admiral Ciliax finally came down in favour of making his dash by the Channel route. He did so on the grounds that the three ships could be closely escorted by destroyers and torpedo boats throughout the passage; that they would be under strong and continuous fighter cover throughout daylight hours from dawn to dusk; that the ships could make full use of the long, dark February nights to cloak much of their passage through the Channel; that a comparatively short dash up Channel would have more chance of success through the element of surprise, and finally that the ship's companies lacked adequate training to undertake a much longer passage round the north of the British Isles. He saw Hitler and explained his outline plan, and left Hitler's headquarters with the Führer's blessing.

This reasoning by Vice-Admiral Ciliax in favour of the Channel route was, it will be noticed, very much in line with the reasoning which had lain behind the Admiralty's appreciation of February 2nd (see Chapter 1). It differed in only one respect: the Admiralty, and indeed the Air Ministry, expected the time of sailing of the ships from Brest to be so adjusted as to bring the German squadron to the narrowest, and therefore most dangerous, part of the Channel between Dover and Calais at dawn, or shortly before it, so that there would still be an hour of darkness to help them through that stretch of water. This would have meant leaving Brest in the afternoon, some hours before nightfall. Vice-Admiral Ciliax, however, thought it more important to leave Brest after dark to avoid detection at the outset of his passage. In the British plan this should have made no difference, as the three patrols of ASV-fitted Hudsons were so placed that they must surely detect any break-out after dark, and thus provide sufficient warning to alert the defence forces in plenty of time.

In selecting the route to be taken through the Channel, Vice-Admiral Ciliax had four requirements to be kept in mind. He needed, first, a course which would keep him well clear of the convoy traffic along the French coast. It would have been easy enough, of course, to stop the sailing of all coastal convoys during the period of the passage, but he decided against this because to do so would suggest to a great many people that an important naval movement was

Above: Air Chief Marshal
Sir Philip Joubert, C-in-C
Coastal Command, with his
naval liaison officer.
Right: Air Marshal Sir
Trafford Leigh-Mallory,
who at the time of the
passage of the German
squadron was commanding
No 11 Fighter Group.

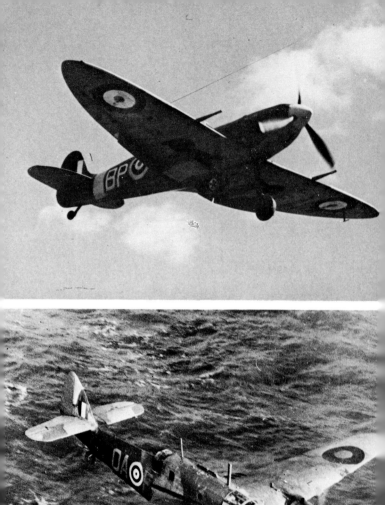

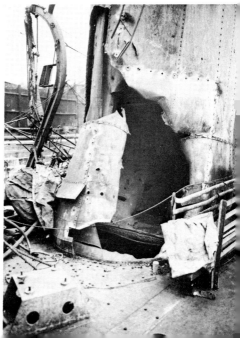

Above left: A Spitfire
fighter.

Left: A Beaufort torpedo
bomber.

Above: The wardroom of
HMS *Worcester* after the
action.

Right: Damage to the deck
and after funnel of HMS
Worcester caused by hits
sustained during the
destroyer action.

Above left: The bridge of
HMS *Worcester* damaged
during the action.
Left: HMS *Worcester* with,
astern of her, HMS
Walpole.
Above: British motor
gunboats in the Channel.
Right: Admiral Sir Bertram
Ramsay.

Above: A German E-boat.
Left: Rear-Admiral
Friedrich Ruge, who was in
charge of German
minesweeping along the
route taken by the
Scharnhorst, Gneisenau and
Prinz Eugen.
Above right: British motor
gunboats in Dover harbour.
Right: A British motor
torpedo boat at speed.

Top: British motor gunboats in the English Channel.
Above: The British minelayer HMS *Welshman,* which laid several minefields across the route taken by the German squadron.

Lt-Commander Eugene Esmonde, second from left, who was awarded a posthumous Victoria Cross for his gallantry during the Swordfish attack on the *Scharnhorst* and *Gneisenau*. On the far right is Ldg Airman A. L. Johnson, who was the rear-gunner in Sub-Lt Rose's Swordfish.

Naval Swordfish torpedo-bombers in flight.

Above left: Beaufort torpedo-bombers being loaded up at a Royal Naval Air Station.
Left: Halifax bombers over Brest. Smoke can be seen rising from a bomb hit on the *Gneisenau* in the right-hand drydock.
Above: This picture taken by a photographic reconnaissance aircraft shows the *Prinz Eugen* in dry-dock.

PRINCE EUGEN

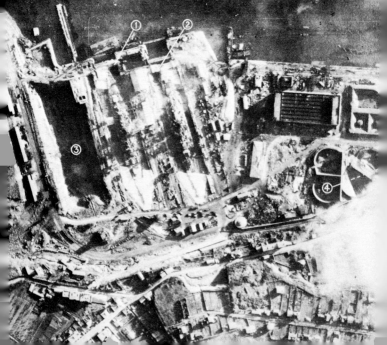

Left: The *Prinz Eugen,* under her camouflage nets, photographed in dock at Brest.

Below left: The *Scharnhorst* (1) and *Gneisenau* (2) in dock at Brest. A new dry-dock (3) is under construction. Oil tanks in the dockyard (4) can be seen burned out after bomb hits.

Right: The guns of the *Prinz Eugen* firing at a Swordfish during the torpedo bomber attack.

Below: Captain Brinkmann, of the *Prinz Eugen,* during the passage up Channel of the German squadron.

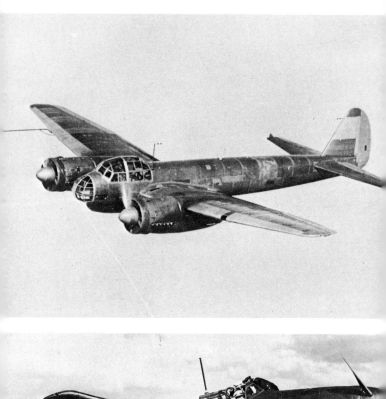

Left: A Junkers Ju 88 in flight.
Below left: A Junkers Ju 87B.
Right: A Swordfish dropping a torpedo.
Below: Messerschmitt Bf 109F fighters.

The cruiser *Prinz Eugen* at Brest in 1941.

imminent, and so he would lose the element of surprise. His course, too, must be clear of all minefields. A third requirement was to plot his course as far as possible beyond the range of the British coastal radar stations, and his fourth and final requirement was deep water so that the ships could maintain a high speed throughout this passage from Brest to Brunsbuttel.

As laid down on the chart the planned course took the ships five miles west of Ushant and then up Channel in deep water to the mouth of the River Somme on a course which was never less than 35 miles from the British coastline. The course then passed east of the Vergoyer Bank and up the French coast to pass three miles off Boulogne and one and a half miles off Cap Gris Nez and so north-easterly through the Dover Straits and out into the North Sea. It was then plotted to pass between the Outer Ruytingen and Sandettié Banks and to follow the Belgian and Dutch coastline keeping about seventeen miles offshore. The ports of Cherbourg, Le Havre, Flushing and Hook of Holland were selected as ports of refuge along the route in case of need and these were warned to stand by to receive the ships if any emergency arose.

The immediate close escort from Brest was to be seven destroyers, to be augmented on passage by the 2nd Torpedo Boat Flotilla from Le Havre which was to join at Point 'Q' (50°N, 0°31'E), by the 3rd Torpedo Boat Flotilla from Dunkirk to join off Cap Gris Nez, and by the 5th Torpedo Boat Flotilla from Flushing to join off the Dutch coast. The 2nd, 4th, and 6th E-boat Flotillas were to join off Cap Gris Nez. In the event, the destroyer escort was reduced to six, as the *Bruno Heinemann,* on her way to Brest on January 25th was sunk by a mine in a field laid by HMS *Plover* a day or two earlier. The composition of these escort forces were:

Destroyers: *Z.29* (Captain D), *Richard Beitzen* (senior officer 5th Destroyer Flotilla), *Jacobi, Friedrich Ihn, Hermann Schoemann,* and *Z.25.*

2nd Torpedo Boat Flotilla: *T.2, T.4, T.5, T.11,* and *T.12.*

| 3rd Torpedo Boat Flotilla: | *T.13, T.14, T.15, T.16,* and *T.17.* |
| 5th Torpedo Boat Flotilla: | *Kondor, Falke, Seeadler, Iltis,* and *Jaguar.* |

The operational control from on shore was vested in Group West, with headquarters in Paris, and Group North, with headquarters at Kiel, whose task it was to sail the various escort forces as and when required to join the squadron and to warn the ports of refuge to be prepared for any emergency action. As soon as the escort forces were at sea they were to come under the operational control of Vice-Admiral Ciliax with his flag in the *Scharnhorst.* In addition to all these arrangements, tugs and salvage gear were distributed in various French, Belgian and Dutch harbours along the planned route.

The actual date of the break-out from Brest would depend on the weather forecast at the time of sailing and for two days ahead, and a party of meteorologists was embarked in the *Gneisenau* for this purpose. Three U-boats were taken off convoy attack duties in the eastern Atlantic and detailed to send weather reports three times daily, from which the forecasts were prepared. After the successful conclusion of the operation, in fact, these meteorologists claimed that it was their accurate forecasting that played the most important part in the preparation and planning of the operation, and there can be no doubt that Vice-Admiral Ciliax was, as a result, able to select his day of departure with considerable confidence that the weather would, on the whole, be on his side.

Air cover for the operation was in the hands of the 3rd Luftflotte under Generalfeldmarschall Sperrle, with twin headquarters at Le Touquet and Schipol, control passing from one to the other as the ships progressed along their planned route. The major part of the daylight fighter cover would, of course, fall on Le Touquet, and Colonel Galland who was in direct control of the provision of fighter cover had his headquarters there. He could call on 250 day fighters and 30 night fighters. Throughout the hours of daylight a minimum of sixteen fighters would be per manently overhead to provide close cover, and an overlap during squadron reliefs would provide for 32 fighters in attendance for ten minutes in every half hour. Reserve squadrons of fighters, for use if the scale of attack developed beyond the capacity of the operational fighters to control, were stationed at Hamsteede, Octeville, Caxyde and St Trond. The night fighters were to be overhead after the ships had rounded Ushant and were on their course up Channel, not more than two at a time because of the difficulties of controlling them in darkness, and to continue cover until relieved by the first squadron of day fighters just before dawn. Fighter control officers were embarked on both the battle-cruisers and the *Prinz Eugen* to ensure that the whole operation of fighter cover went without a hitch.

In addition to the fighter cover, Fliegerkorps IX was to be prepared to send out bombers to attack any British ships which might attempt to deny the passage of the battle-cruisers and also to carry out a diversionary raid on Portsmouth during the early morning of the day selected for the passage of the English Channel. Reconnaissance and sea service aircraft were also detailed for duty as required.

Considerable attention was also paid to the problem of jamming the British coastal radar stations during the actual passage of the ships. It was considered that a sudden and complete jamming would inevitably alert the British to the fact that a major operation or movement was taking place, although it was also a requirement that, while the ships were within radar range from Britain, jamming must be continuous. A programme was worked out to operate over several days whereby the period of jamming each morning was increased each day so that, it was hoped, suspicions would not be aroused when, at the time of the actual passage, it became continuous and heavy. This, in fact, is what occurred, and those officers on watch in the fighter stations in Britain whose suspicions were aroused by the volume of jamming during the morning of February 12th were generally thought to be scaremongers and their opinions disregarded.

The minesweeping schedules were arranged so that the whole of the planned route was swept in such a manner that it would be impossible for any observer to connect them with the passage from Brest of the Atlantic squadron. The planned route was swept in portions unconnected with each other but so designed that the last portions swept filled in the whole of the final route. All the minesweeping was done during the hours of darkness to deny to the British all knowledge of the operation, and on the night of February 11th-12th individual minesweepers were sailed from various ports along the French, Belgian, Dutch and German coasts to anchor themselves in pre-determined positions where they would act as mark-boats to assist the squadron with its navigational problems. In addition, two or three minesweeping flotillas were held at instant readiness during that same night in case there should be a last-minute discovery of a new minefield. The wisdom of this additional precaution was amply demonstrated when, during the night of February 11th-12th, the minefield laid off Etaples by HMS *Welshman* in the early morning of February 8th was discovered only just in time, and there was a full minesweeping flotilla ready at hand to sweep a channel through it.

So far as the planned route, bordering the coasts of France, Belgium, and Holland was concerned, the most meticulous planning to cover every conceivable contingency had taken place. But oddly enough it did not extend to Germany itself, where much was left to be decided on an *ad hoc* basis. The German naval authorities, including Vice-Admiral Ciliax himself, expected to arrive in German home waters with at least one of the three big ships, and possibly all three, damaged and in need of assistance, but none of the dry-docks at Kiel or Wilhelmshafen were specially earmarked or prepared for their reception, and fleet tugs were not ordered to be standing by for them on their arrival. Relief escort forces were not provided to take over the duty of bringing the ships safely into port, an odd omission when it was confidently expected that the existing destroyers and torpedo boats would have gone through day-long battle against a heavy British attack. Nor were any additional navigational aids provided to assist the big ships through the difficult coastal waters of the Elbe and Jad estuaries although it was known they would be arriving at night and possibly damaged. In the event, this turned out to be the most difficult part of the whole passage as the *Scharnhorst* and *Gneisenau,* both damaged by mines, had to feel their way into port without assistance.

The whole of the detailed planning was carried out under the most intense secrecy throughout and with a full quota of deception and cover plans. Beyond the captains and navigating officers of the two battle-cruisers and the *Prinz Eugen,* no one on board any of the ships had knowledge of the proposal to sail the three ships home to Germany. The arrival in Brest, shortly before the planned date of the break-out, of the destroyers which were to form the close escort, and the establishment on board of the German Air Force officers who were to act as fighter control officers, were explained as preparations for a big combined naval and air force exercise in the Bay of Biscay, and to fortify this explanation, battle-practice targets were ordered to be prepared in St Nazaire and La Pallice for concentrated gunnery practice. A small proportion of the ships' companies of the *Scharnhorst, Gneisenau,* and *Prinz Eugen* were even sent home on leave as an additional indication that the three ships were to continue their stay in Brest. Every ship in the escort was given sealed orders which were to be opened only at a given signal when they were at sea. These orders contained the full details of the operation.

On the minesweeping front, only Rear-Admiral Ruge, who was in charge of all minesweeping, and his chief of staff knew of the operation. In one or two cases, German minefields needed to be swept to fit the navigational plan for the squadron; these were covered by false reports of British minelaying in those areas. The movement to Brest of the destroyers to form the close escort was also used as an excuse to sweep waters through which they might pass.

Similar secrecy was exercised with the arrangements for the continuous fighter cover required by the squadron. The proposed joint exercises in the Bay of Biscay was an excuse to cover the increased training of fighter pilots in operating with ships which the actual passage would call for, and as the day of the break-out approached, the squadrons were informed that a valuable convoy being passed eastward through the Channel was to be protected. At no time before the passage were the pilots informed of the constitution of the convoy, but each was briefed fully just before take-off on what they might expect to see in the Channel on the actual morning of the operation.

As a final cover plan, information was widely disseminated of a large dinner party to be held in Paris by the admiral commanding Group West, to be followed the next morning by a shooting party at Rambouillet. As soon as the date of the departure of the Brest squadron was fixed, invitation cards were printed, and among those who received them were 30 officers stationed in Brest, mainly on board the *Scharnhorst, Gneisenau* and *Prinz Eugen.* The dinner was announced as at 20.30 hrs on February 11th to be followed by the shooting party on the 12th, and sporting guns were delivered on board the ships to those officers who did not have their own with them.

The overall outline of the plan was almost entirely the work of Vice-Admiral Ciliax, but within it there were still some unknowns. One of these was the degree of success which the Royal Air Force might achieve during the days before the ships were due to leave. The attack on January 6th, 1942, in which the *Gneisenau* was damaged (see Introduction) was a pointer to the possibilities. It was finally decided, in conjunction with Hitler himself, that if one battle-cruiser were damaged in a raid, the other would make the attempt in company with the *Prinz Eugen,* but that if both were damaged, the *Prinz Eugen* was not to proceed on her own.

Ciliax's next preoccupation was with the training of the crews of the three ships. They had been so long in Brest, and had spent so much of the time in dry-dock, that there had been little or no opportunity for any worthwhile sea time for the men. In accordance with the general German naval practice, ships' companies did not live on board their ships when in harbour but in barracks ashore, and therefore lacked the "feel" of the ships in which they served. There had also been a considerable dilution of the original crews since their arrival in Brest as key personnel were drafted away to more important duties than sitting-out the air raids on Brest. Within the last month the *Scharnhorst* and *Gneisenau* had had only one day at sea each for engine trials and gunnery practice, the *Scharnhorst* on February 3rd and the *Gneisenau* on January 27th. The *Prinz Eugen* had not even had that, having remained solidly in Brest since her arrival eight months previously on June 1st, 1941. It was not much to go on, but it had to do, as there was no chance of further exercising before the next dark period when the attempt had to be made.

The date and time of departure was already fixed within certain limits. The dark period, five days either side of the new moon was from February 10th to 20th. If the ships were to leave Brest in the evening, to shield their departure from the British reconnaissance aircraft which flew frequent missions over Brest, an east-running tide during the early morning hours was desirable, not only to help the ships on their way but to give them deeper water along their route. A day with high water at Dover around 09.00 hrs or 09.30 hrs would give them the best of the tide for their purpose. On February 12th, nicely within the dark period, the time of high water at Dover was 09.30 hrs, and if that date corresponded with a favourable weather forecast in the Channel and southern North Sea, it would be ideal for the purpose. Moonrise was at 05.52 hrs on the 12th, so that maximum darkness was assured.

The meteorologists in the *Gneisenau,* basing their long-range forecasts on the information supplied by the three weather U-boats in the eastern Atlantic, predicted to Vice-Admiral Ciliax that on the night of February 11th the wind would be westerly, force 3-4, the sea slight to moderate, and visibility up to about five miles. These conditions were likely to continue through the forenoon of the 12th, but would deteriorate rapidly in the afternoon with cloud increasing to ten-tenths at 2,000ft, the wind rising to force 6-7 and creating a heavy swell from the westward, with visibility decreasing steadily to a maximum of about two miles. These were the ideal conditions for a hazardous operation of this nature, reasonably good weather with a favourable tide during the dark hours while the main run up Channel was being made and then deteriorating apace during the period when attacks by the British were most likely to be anticipated. Vice-Admiral Ciliax therefore decided that February 11th was to be the date of departure from Brest, with the passage of the English Channel on the 12th. He fixed the hour of departure at 19.30 hrs, which answered his requirement of leaving harbour after all daylight had faded.

He decided to work on the assumption that the ships and their escort would steam at a speed of 25 knots, and using this speed, to which was added the assistance from the east-running tide, a detailed timetable was worked out for the planned route, marking off times and positions where the additional escorts of three torpedo boat and three E-boat flotillas were to join the force. He allowed for up to two hours' delay in his time of departure to take care of any last-minute complications (one did in the event occur with an evening air raid on Brest by the Royal Air Force), confident that he could make up for time lost initially by increasing the speed of advance of the squadron. His operational orders to the *Gneisenau* and *Prinz Eugen* were drawn up on these precise lines, and they included an order that if any one ship was hit and disabled, or slowed down, the other two were to disregard her and continue on their course at maximum speed.

Vice-Admiral Ciliax had still one more card to play. He requested that on the night of February 11th a flotilla of E-boats should be despatched to the neighbourhood of Dover to draw out, and if possible damage, the Dover motor torpedo boats. Eight of them operated for most of the night in the area of Dungeness, but Vice-Admiral Ramsay was not drawn, committing only his motor gunboats to the battle and requesting aircraft to assist by dropping flares. The E-boats withdrew in the early morning, without contributing anything to the forthcoming battle.

In a final bid to ensure secrecy all the operational orders were issued under five codenames. It was only when the final commitment to proceed was made that the actual codename was released. It was *Cerberus*.

CHAPTER THREE

The Break-through

As has been seen, the detailed German plan envisaged the three ships, with their six destroyers as escorts, clearing Brest at 19.30 hrs on the 11th, leaving Ushant five miles on their starboard hand, and then turning up Channel on a course which would keep them well clear of the local convoy traffic along the French coast. The speed of advance was to be 25 knots, to bring them through the Straits of Dover at 11.30 hrs in the forenoon of the 12th. This detailed and rigid planning was necessary to ensure that the passage of the ships coincided with the minesweeping routines to clear their planned track.

The operation did not go exactly as planned, as just after the ships had slipped and were getting under way in Brest Harbour, an air-raid alarm was sounded. For a time it looked as though the operation would have to be postponed, but just over an hour and a half later the all-clear was given, and by adjusting the speed of advance to 27 knots the time lost at the start could be regained by the time the ships reached the vital stage of their passage, the Straits of Dover. The German force, with the *Scharnhorst* leading, followed by the *Gneisenau* and then the *Prinz Eugen,* were clear of the net barrage at Brest and heading out to sea at 17 knots, working up to 27 knots just before midnight. The two British submarines operating off Brest, the modern *Sealion* and the elderly *H.34,* normally used only for training purposes, did not sight the German ships since, of course, they had to withdraw to seaward at night in order to come to the surface and recharge their batteries.

Twelve minutes after midnight on February 11th/12th, and 72 minutes behind their scheduled time, the German force rounded Ushant and altered course for the English

41

Channel. They had settled down at 27 knots, the night was very dark but clear with scattered clouds and a light breeze from the south-west. The moon, in its last quarter was due to rise just before 06.00 hrs on the 12th so there would be no dissipation of the darkness of the night. The tide had begun to make up-Channel, to give them an extra two or three knots of speed and the prospect of deeper water over any minefields which might have been missed by the German minesweepers. Behind them, it was a noisy night at Brest as a heavy raid by Royal Air Force bombers attacked their empty berths. All had gone very fortunately.

Just how fortunately it had gone was not fully known either to Vice-Admiral Ciliax in the *Scharnhorst* or yet, unhappily, to Vice-Admiral Ramsay in his headquarters at Dover. A vital part of the system set up to give early warning of the movement of the German ships from Brest were the three night air patrols flown throughout the hours of darkness by Hudsons of Coastal Command fitted with ASV (radar) sets. These early sets were relatively inefficient in comparison with the sets developed later in the war but they were in theory, at least, capable of detecting a large ship at a range of 30 miles.

The most westerly of these patrols, known as the "Stopper" patrol, was flown off the entrance to Brest itself. The first aircraft took off from St Eval, in Cornwall, at 18.27 hrs, but 40 minutes later the Hudson encountered a German Ju88 night fighter, and while evading it the radar set was switched off. As soon as it was switched on again it was found to be dead, and after some minutes trying to make it work without success, the Hudson returned. The time it left its patrol line was 19.40 hrs. After landing at St Eval, 40 minutes were spent in trying to locate the fault, but as it could not be located, the pilot was ordered to take up another Hudson. This one refused to start, and it took another 50 minutes to find the cause. Both faults were discovered at about the same time. In the case of the first Hudson, the ASV fuse had blown because the "cold" set had been switched on again with full power instead of half power; the second Hudson's refusal to start was because of a damp sparking plug. By this time another Hudson was on the way to "Stopper" patrol. It arrived at 22.38 hrs but for three hours "Stopper" had been unwatched and during that time the German ships had left Brest and were rounding Ushant.

The next patrol line, known as the "Line SE" patrol, was between Ushant and the Ile de Bréhat. The first Hudson took off at 18.48 hrs and reached its patrol line at 19.40 hrs. When the ASV set was switched on it refused to function. For one and a half hours the crew of the Hudson tried to trace the fault, but were unable to find it. The darkness of the night made any attempt at visual reconnaissance hopeless, so at 21.13 hrs, the pilot broke radio silence to report the failure and was ordered to return. No relief aircraft was sent out, and for the rest of the night "Line SE" was left unwatched. The German ships passed along it between 01.00 hrs and 04.00 hrs on the morning of the 12th.

The third patrol line, known as the "Habo" patrol, was flown between Le Havre and Boulogne, the Hudsons operating from Thorney Island. The first aircraft flew its normal patrol and reported nothing: the second, relieving it, was ordered to fly only two circuits of the patrol as there was a thick mist in the Channel which the Station Controller at Thorney Island thought might turn into fog and make landing difficult. As a result the Hudson left the "Habo" patrol at 06.15 hrs instead of the normal time of 07.15 hrs. Had the extra hour been flown, the German battle-cruisers would have been off Le Havre, and within range of the "Habo" ASV.

These three gaps in the patrols were unfortunate, as all of them corresponded with the actual passage of the German ships. But what was more unfortunate still was the fact that the breakdowns and curtailments were not reported to the naval operational headquarters at Dover, which was left in the belief that all patrols had been flown normally and that no movements had been detected. It is arguable that had the Dover headquarters been warned of the failures it might well have been alerted to the possibility that the German ships were in fact making their expected move. It might well, too, have brought the naval forces, including the Fleet Air Arm Swordfish, to immediate notice instead of reverting to the

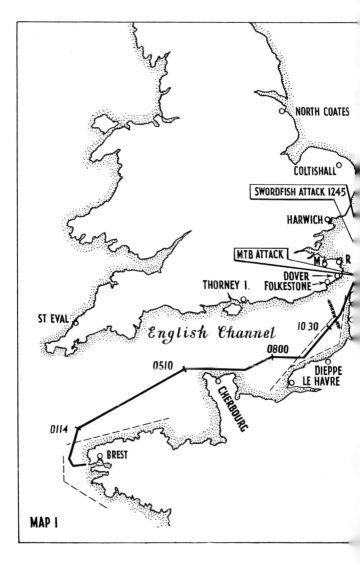

NORTH COATES

COLTISHALL

SWORDFISH ATTACK 1245

HARWICH

MTB ATTACK   M6   R

DOVER
FOLKESTONE

THORNEY I.

ST. EVAL

English Channel

10.30

0800

0510

DIEPPE
LE HAVRE

CHERBOURG

0114

BREST

MAP I

44

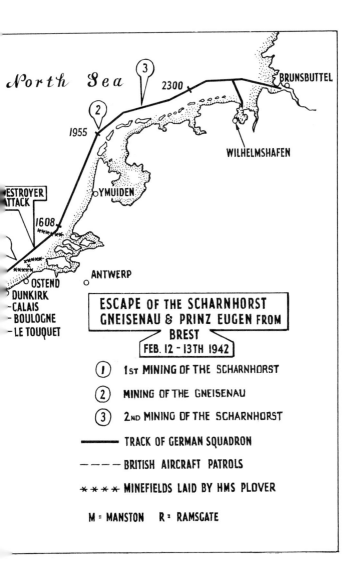

North Sea

BRUNSBUTTEL

2300

WILHELMSHAFEN

YMUIDEN

DESTROYER
ATTACK

1608

OSTEND
DUNKIRK
CALAIS
BOULOGNE
LE TOUQUET

ANTWERP

**ESCAPE OF THE SCHARNHORST
GNEISENAU & PRINZ EUGEN FROM
BREST**
FEB. 12 - 13TH 1942

① 1ST MINING OF THE SCHARNHORST

② MINING OF THE GNEISENAU

③ 2ND MINING OF THE SCHARNHORST

────── TRACK OF GERMAN SQUADRON

──── BRITISH AIRCRAFT PATROLS

✱✱✱✱ MINEFIELDS LAID BY HMS PLOVER

M = MANSTON   R = RAMSGATE

usual four hours' notice which was the normal procedure when the night had passed without incident or report. It is possible, too, that a knowledge of the gaps in the patrols might have drawn some additional attention to the operations of a group of eight German E-boats against British shipping off Dungeness during the night of February 11th/12th (see Chapter 2). E-boat operations in the Channel were not all that uncommon, but these remained out all night, which was contrary to the usual pattern of normal anti-shipping strikes. The headquarters at Dover, if alerted to the possibility that the German ships from Brest could be on the move, might have thought that the intentions of the E-boats were to draw out the British motor torpedo boats and tire them out before the German ships passed the Narrows, and thus be doubly on their guard.

All this time the German ships were steaming steadily up Channel gradually catching up on the time lost at the start. All was going like clockwork. The first two squadrons of fighters from the 3rd Luftflotte duly arrived at 07.30 hrs on the morning of the 12th to provide the stipulated air cover, which would remain overhead during daylight hours. As they came abreast of Fécamp at 09.15 hrs the 2nd and 3rd Torpedo Boat Flotillas, each with five boats, joined the six destroyers to augment the surface escort.

As daylight began to flood the Channel, look-outs in the German ships were doubled. All on board, from Vice-Admiral Ciliax downwards, recognised that wonderfully good fortune had brought them through the night unobserved, and that any moment now would bring British reconnaissance planes overhead and, within minutes of being recognised, attack from sea and air. But the minutes sped by, no British aircraft appeared above the ships, and the crucial area of the passage, the narrow strait between Dover and Calais, was getting ever nearer. It seemed to the Germans to be too good to be true. They closed the French shore slightly to be off Dieppe at 09.45 hrs, and at 10.25 hrs slowed temporarily to ten knots to cross one of the minefields laid by HMS *Welshman*. This was the field to the west of Etaples, unfortunately discovered by the German 1st Minesweeping Flotilla shortly after the three big ships had left Brest on February 11th. Sweeping through the night, a narrow channel had been cleared through the minefield and markboats moored to show the limits of the swept area. The other three fields laid by the *Welshman* were not on the actual track taken by the *Scharnhorst* and her companions. Once through the minefields the speed of advance was again increased to 27 knots and at 11.56 hrs the force rounded Cap Gris Nez, following the swept channel again conveniently shown by minesweepers moored in position to serve as markboats. They were now midway between Boulogne and Calais, and although Vice-Admiral Ciliax knew that their presence in the English Channel was no longer a secret to the British (see below), he was fortified by the arrival of the 5th Torpedo Boat Flotilla and three flotillas of E-boats (2nd, 4th, and 6th) to augment his surface escort. He deployed the E-boat flotillas to seaward of the squadron and ordered them to make smoke. At the same time further squadrons of fighters arrived overhead to double the air cover through the narrower stretches of their passage. Bomber and reconnaissance aircraft also arrived overhead to add to the precautionary measures to protect the ships. More than an hour had passed since Vice-Admiral Ciliax knew he had been discovered, and as yet none of the expected attacks had materialised.

Because of the stepping up of jamming by the Germans along the French coast there appeared to be nothing unusual to the British in a particularly long morning of jamming on February 12th. One by one reports came in of the usual interference from all the radar stations along the coast. Nevertheless, before the jamming started, they were picking up indications of an unusual amount of air activity, which were reported both to No 11 Fighter Group Headquarters at Hornchurch and naval headquarters at Newhaven, but neither took much notice. Air movements did not concern the navy; at 11 Group it was thought to be an air-sea rescue operation or the escorting of a coastal convoy.

In some of the British radar stations the new short-wave Type 271 set had replaced the older sets, and these as yet were incapable of being jammed. By 08.30 hrs several plots had come in to Fighter Command headquarters at Stanmore which appeared to indicate a number of aircraft circling in a small area. At the same time the radar station at Swingate, near Dover, which also had the Type 271 set, plotted groups of aircraft north of Le Havre, and held them in a continuous plot for over an hour. They were in fact the day fighters coming out to take over continuous cover of the German squadron as it passed up Channel. At Swingate the plots were interpreted as aircraft circling over ships steaming eastward at a speed of approximately 25 knots.

At 10.16 hrs something else appeared on the radar plot at Swingate. They were three large "blips" in the vicinity of Boulogne at a range of 56 miles. They were too large to be the usual small Channel shipping, and for the first time a suspicion was aroused in the minds of three or four men that something unusual was happening. One of them was the station commander at Swingate, who tried to get through to Dover to report his suspicions. His direct line failed to produce a reply, and when he tried the scrambler line it was equally unresponsive. It was later discovered that both had been plugged simultaneously into the same line, making both inoperative. He eventually got his report through via Portsmouth.

Another man whose suspicions were being aroused was the Controller of the filter room at Fighter Command, who had been studying the plots, and talked to 11 Group headquarters about them. 11 Group still considered the plots either as an air-sea rescue operation or German aircraft exercising. When the Fighter Command Controller talked about the possibility of the plot being the *Scharnhorst* and *Gneisenau,* his theory was disregarded.

A third suspicious man was the Controller at the fighter station at Biggin Hill. He too had plotted the radar reports and came to the conclusion that they indicated a group of ships steaming at 25 knots. Knowing that this could be no coastal convoy, he telephoned to 11 Group to say that in his opinion this was *Fuller* in operation. No one at 11 Group appeared to know what *Fuller* meant. It appeared later that the operation had been considered so secret that the

48

code-name had been revealed only to one or two top-ranking officers. Fortunately the Biggin Hill Controller, realising that *Fuller* meant nothing to 11 Group, also rang up the fighter station at Hawkinge and asked for a special reconnaissance.

A fourth officer whose suspicions had been aroused by the radar plots was the air liaison officer at Vice-Admiral Ramsay's Dover headquarters. In addition to asking for an additional Spitfire reconnaissance at 10.45 hrs (in fact unnecessary as one was at that moment being flown) he rang up Manston and warned the commander of No. 825 Squadron of the Fleet Air Arm (Lt-Commander Esmonde) to bring his aircraft to immediate readiness, loading torpedoes set to run deep. It showed a considerable presence of mind that, as early as this, he had not only recognised the possibility that the radar plot might be the German squadron steaming up Channel but had also taken concrete steps to prepare for the possibility.

In the meantime the normal day reconnaissance ("Jim Crow") flights were under way, scheduled to take place every two hours throughout daylight hours from dawn onwards. The first of them reported, on its return, an empty sea at least so far as the German battle-cruisers were concerned. There were, as noticed above in Chapter 1, orders in force that radio silence must be observed during these flights on the outward flight, except in emergency, and in accordance with this the "Jim Crow" pilots only described what they had seen on their debriefing. The first pilot reported seeing one E-boat leaving Boulogne. The second reported sighting eleven small vessels east of Ostend and a further six east of Zeebrugge. As a result of these sightings, 11 Group ordered a shipping strike to be flown against the group of ships off Ostend.

As a result of the Biggin Hill Controller's request to Hawkinge at 10.00 hrs, a second reconnaissance was ordered at 10.10 hrs and took off at 10.20 hrs. Both Spitfire pilots saw a group of 20-30 vessels off Boulogne, with an escort of five destroyers, which they took to be a coastal convoy. They also saw nine E-boats to the north-west of the convoy. The Spitfires returned to Hawkinge and landed at 10.50 hrs. The first pilot reported the convoy, which was confirmed by the second pilot who also stated that he saw a ship with a tripod mast. When shown a copy of *Jane's Fighting Ships,* he identified what he saw as the *Scharnhorst.* His identification was not taken seriously at 11 Group headquarters. The sighting of the convoy was reported to naval headquarters at Dover but no mention was made of the ship with a tripod mast.

During this time another flight of two Spitfires was taking place over the Channel, in the nature of a "private venture" by Group Captain Beamish and Squadron Leader Boyd in search of targets of opportunity to shoot up. At 10.42 hrs they came out of low cloud and saw beneath them the whole German squadron. They dived through the German "flak" to escape the fighters covering the squadron, knowing that these could not follow through the German gunfire, raced across the bows of the big ships at little above sea level, and made for home. Group Captain Beamish, unfortunately, made no report of what he had seen by R/T even though, in the orders about wireless silence he had himself laid down, it was to be broken in an emergency. The two Spitfires landed at 11.09 hrs. Confirmation that the German force from Brest was at sea was passed by 11 Group to Fighter Command headquarters, thence to the Air Ministry, by them to the Admiralty, and so to Dover, reaching Vice-Admiral Ramsay's headquarters at 11.25 hrs. The coast artillery was informed and at 12.10 hrs the 9.2in battery on the South Foreland opened fire, with spotting and control by radar as the ships themselves were invisible in the low cloud and behind their smoke screen. The opening range was 27,000 yards and 33 rounds were fired. There were no hits.

When the first shells landed in the sea astern of the *Prinz Eugen* the German ships were about ten miles west of Calais, steering north-east and still steaming at 27 knots. They could now expect almost continuous attack from the sea and the air for the remainder of the passage home. So far Vice-Admiral Ciliax had enjoyed remarkable fortune in the execution of his plan, far better than he had ever expected, and his meteorological officer on board encouraged him further with a forecast of rapidly deteriorating weather over the southern North Sea, with a rising wind, a rough sea, and cloud increasing to about ten-tenths down to 1,500ft. The wind and sea would make the inevitable attacks by destroyers and motor torpedo boats much more chancey affairs than they would have been under good sea conditions; the thickening cloud would help him by making the task of British bombers all the more difficult. But if he could expect to be attacked from now on, at least he was more than half-way home and the relatively short period of daylight left made his chances of success so much greater than they might well have been.

At Dover, on receipt of the 11.25 hrs' signal from the Admiralty confirming that the German ships were at sea, Vice-Admiral Ramsay was putting his part of the combined operation smoothly into operation. The striking force of five motor torpedo boats and two motor gunboats from Dover, and the three motor torpedo boats from Ramsgate were at once ordered to sea, and a signal sent to Harwich to bring the destroyer striking force to immediate notice: they should have reverted to four hours' notice at 07.00 hrs. Fortunately they were already at sea exercising off the Suffolk coast, and a signal to them to proceed in execution of their previous orders was enough to send them on their way at full speed. And thanks to the previous warning at 10.45 hrs by the air liaison officer to No 825 Squadron at Manston, the naval torpedo bombers were also ready. Lt-Commander Esmonde was impatient to be on his way but was told to wait until a fighter escort had been arranged. A request for this was telephoned from Dover to Fighter Command and 11 Group headquarters for as strong an escort as could be managed, since because of their slow speed Swordfish aircraft were very vulnerable. Ten minutes later the Controller at 11 Group replied that he had made arrangements for three squadrons of Spitfires from Biggin Hill to provide the close cover and two more squadrons to attack just ahead of the Swordfish as 'anti-flak' squadrons. All these were to rendezvous with the Swordfish over the airfield at Manston at 12.20 hrs, which would give good time for the Swordfish to get their attack in before the enemy ships were through the straits and beginning to open out the distance. At the same time, two additional squadrons from Hornchurch would be sent direct to the scene of operations to provide further cover both for the Swordfish and the motor torpedo boats during their attacks. All this would give a total of 84 fighters at the scene of the attack.

While these arrangements were being made, the Senior Air Staff Officer at No 16 Group, Coastal Command, telephoned to Dover to suggest that the Swordfish attack be delayed by an hour and a half so that it could be combined with a torpedo attack by Beauforts of Coastal Command. The suggestion had to be turned down for four reasons:

1 That a great advantage would be gained if the enemy could be crippled by torpedo hits as early as possible. Once he reached the area of the sandbanks off the Belgian coast no torpedo attack was possible until he emerged into deep water again some 80-90 miles from Manston.

2 An attack at this distance would entail a flight of 2½ hours for the Swordfish, exposed the whole time to continuous attack by the enemy shore-based fighters. With such a flight, their fighter escort would also need to be relieved by a second escort in a position where it might be difficult to make contact. Nor would there be any economy in fighter escorts, as the different speeds of the two types of torpedo bombers, 150 knots for Beauforts, 80 knots for Swordfish, would inevitably mean separate escort forces.

3 It was desirable for the Swordfish to make their attack within radar cover from Britain to ensure that they could find the target without having to 'make a search for it, particularly in view of the deteriorating weather with reducing visibility.

4 Between 12.30 hrs and 13.30 hrs the maximum number of British fighters would be in the area, and because of the vulnerability of the Swordfish and the very hazardous nature of their task, the more fighters that were available the better would be their chance of success.

It was unfortunate—in his official report Vice-Admiral Ramsay described it as a "major tragedy"—that the majority of the fighters assigned to escort the Swordfish failed to arrive over Manston. Esmonde's time of attack had been set at 12.45 hrs, to coincide as near as possible with that of the motor torpedo boats and motor gunboats from Dover and Ramsgate, and he was impatient to be off. By 12.28 hrs only ten of the 36 fighters had arrived, and Esmonde decided that he could wait no longer. He set his course for the estimated position of the enemy, 23 miles 140° from Ramsgate, approximately halfway between Calais and Dunkirk, hoping to fill some of the gaps in his fighter cover with the two squadrons of Spitfires from Hornchurch which had been ordered direct to the scene of operations. Unfortunately these two squadrons were ordered to search too far to the westward, never sighted the enemy, and took no part in the action.

The five motor torpedo boats and two motor gunboats from Dover, which had left harbour at 11.55 hrs, settled down at 36 knots on an east-south-easterly course expecting to intercept the enemy between Calais and Dunkirk. They were led by Lt-Commander E. N. Pumphrey in MTB 221, and at 12.10 hrs he sighted two large patches of smoke on his starboard bow. This was the smoke-screen which Vice-Admiral Ciliax had ordered his E-boats to lay shortly after rounding Cap Gris Nez. Soon afterwards he sighted two flotillas of E-boats, each disposed in two divisions in line ahead, with a gap of about half a mile between the flotillas. There was no sight yet of the three heavy ships, but Pumphrey knew that they must be hidden by the smoke. He closed the E-boats on a converging course, engaging them at a range of about 1,000 yards. As the range closed he sighted the shape of big ships behind the smoke, two battle-cruisers followed by a heavy cruiser, and knew he had found his target. They were some 4,000 yards (two miles) beyond the E-boats and he estimated their speed at 23 knots. He made an enemy sighting report, timed 12.23 hrs, to Dover and increased to maximum speed in order to cross ahead of the E-boat line and attack from inside the screen.

It was as he was working up to full speed that one of his engines failed. The fault was found and rectified almost immediately, but it was evident to Pumphrey that his plan to cross ahead of the leading E-boats and get inside the screen could not succeed, for not only were the E-boats more heavily armed than the British motor torpedo boats but they were also faster by two or three knots. He therefore decided to try to go through the screen in the gap between the two E-boat flotillas. At this moment his engines again developed a fault and his speed dropped to 15 knots. He ordered the remainder of his motor torpedo boats to continue the attack independently while he took MTB 221 in on a closing course to try to reach a firing position for his torpedoes. He got within a range of 800 yards of the E-boats and, finding their fire become increasingly effective and realising that he was in danger of losing MTB 221 before getting his torpedoes away, he fired them at the leading battle-cruiser, which was the *Scharnhorst,* at an estimated range of 3,000 yards.

Of his decision to attack through the screen rather than from inside it, forced upon him by lack of speed in comparison with that of the E-boats, Pumphrey later wrote in his report: "I considered the prospect of success for this manoeuvre to be extremely slight, and wished very much that the MGBs were in support, or that our fighter aircraft were present to attack the E-boat screen. It is considered that with either, or preferably both of these forms of support, the MTB attack might have been a different story. The only fighters present, however, were Germans which attacked the MTBs intermittently . . ." Vice-Admiral Ramsay, however, after comments on the poor capabilities of British motor torpedo boats in comparison with German E boats, both in armament and speed, endorsed the decision to fire torpedoes through the screen. "Outnumbered by E-boats", he wrote in his report, "attacked by destroyers also with a higher speed than their own, and engaged by numerous enemy fighters, it is greatly to their credit that each MTB was able to get in an attack on the heavy ships".

MTB 219 (Temp. Sub-Lieutenant M. Arnold-Forster) had been fairly heavily attacked by German fighters and had for this reason fallen a little astern of station. She and MTB 48 (Lieutenant C. A. Law) had had to take evasive action which had delayed them slightly, but after driving off the fighters with their Lewis guns they again closed the enemy and fired their torpedoes through the gap between the two

E-boat flotillas at an estimated range of 4,000-4,500 yards. These attacks were made between 12.31 hrs and 12.35 hrs.

Lieutenant L. J. H. Gamble (MTB 45) after receiving the order to attack independently, had decided to go round the stern of the E-boat screen and get inside it that way. He quickly discovered that this would take him too far astern to make an effective attack and so he steered for the gap between the two E-boat flotillas. He fired his torpedoes at the *Prinz Eugen* but one of them misfired. By the time the torpedo impulse had been changed, Lieutenant Gamble's problems were increased by the appearance of one of the destroyers which had been with the big ships since leaving Brest, the *Friedrich Ihn,* which Vice-Admiral Ciliax had ordered, with another, to strengthen the E-boats. Gamble attempted to fire his remaining torpedo at the destroyer, but again there was a misfire. MTB 45 therefore disengaged, retiring on a north-easterly course with the *Friedrich Ihn* in pursuit.

It was at this moment that the two motor gunboats from Dover arrived on the scene. They engaged the *Friedrich Ihn* and at the same time laid a smoke-screen to cover the withdrawal of the motor torpedo boats. They, too, were heavily attacked by German fighters throughout.

The fifth motor torpedo boat, MTB 44 (Sub-Lieutenant R. F. Saunders) had been handicapped by a complete breakdown of her starboard engine after turning to try to get through the gap in the E-boat screen. She fell a long way astern of the rest of the flotilla but finally made her way round the stern of the screen. By this time repairs to her engines had restored partial operation and she reached a firing position about 4,000 yards on the beam of the battle-cruisers. At this moment they both altered course 90° to port in order to comb the tracks of the torpedoes fired earlier by the other motor torpedo boats. MTB 44 fired one torpedo at the *Scharnhorst* and the second at the *Prinz Eugen,* which had not made so sharp a turn. She then turned for home and withdrew safely with the other four MTBs and the two MGBs. None of the seven suffered any casualties, none had been extensively damaged, and all made the rendezvous off

55

the South-East Goodwin Buoy at 12.55 hrs, exactly one hour after leaving Dover.

Although the torpedo fired at the *Prinz Eugen* by MTB 44 appeared to hit her under the bridge, throwing up a column of spray, in fact it did not. Pumphrey, in MTB 221, also reported this as a hit. The column of spray which was seen by the motor torpedo boats was probably thrown up by the premature explosion of torpedoes dropped by the Swordfish during their attack, two of which were reported by the *Prinz Eugen* as exploding when they hit the water in her vicinity and before starting their run. For by this time the Swordfish, with their pathetically small fighter escort, had arrived on the scene and were making their gallant attacks.

Esmonde, with his six Swordfish of No 825 Squadron, Fleet Air Arm, had waited for as long as he dared over Manston for the arrival of the three squadrons of Spitfires which he had been told were to form his immediate escort. He had been informed, too, of the four additional squadrons which he could expect to meet over the scene of attack, two to augment his escort and two to prepare the way by attacking the German escort vessels and acting as "anti-flak" aircraft. At 12.28 hrs, eight minutes later than his planned time of departure, Esmonde could wait no longer and set off. As he flew out on the south-easterly course which would bring his Swordfish over the German ships, enemy fighters intercepted him only about ten miles out from Ramsgate, with about twelve miles still to go. The Swordfish were flying in formation of two sub-flights of three aircraft each, the leading sub-flight consisting of Swordfish W.5984, W.5983, and W.5907, piloted respectively by Esmonde, Sub-Lieutenant B. W. Rose and Sub-Lieutenant C. M. Kingsmill, the following sub-flight consisting of Swordfish W.4523, W.5985, and W.5978, of which the pilots were Lieutenant J. C. Thompson, Sub-Lieutenant C. R. Wood and Sub-Lieutenant P. Bligh. Although the Spitfires did their best to keep the enemy fighters away they were unable to prevent them getting among the Swordfish which were incessantly attacked. All three aircraft in the first sub-flight were damaged in the aerial dog-fight, and it is probable that all in the following sub-flight were equally

56

damaged, though there were no survivors among these three to confirm the fact. A further result of this attack was to slow down the rate of approach of the Swordfish slightly by reason of the evasive tactics they were forced to adopt throughout the seven or eight minutes during which the enemy fighters were among them.

The three big enemy ships were sighted through the smoke-screen laid by the E-boats and the leading sub-flight made for them, passing over the destroyer and E-boat screen and through the anti-aircraft fire thrown up by them. This fire was not as intense as it could well have been since there were too many enemy fighters in the vicinity. The small Spitfire escort of ten aircraft was swamped, and the other four squadrons which, according to the initial plan should have been there, had failed to arrive. As Swordfish W.5984 passed over the screen it was seen by the other two Swordfish to have had the lower port main plane almost entirely shot away, and was still being attacked incessantly by enemy fighters. Somehow Esmonde managed to keep it in the air and still flying towards the target. With its maximum speed of 80 knots and its relatively clumsy construction, it was a sitting target for the enemy fighters. When Esmonde had reached a position about 3,000 yards from the *Scharnhorst* and *Gneisenau* his Swordfish was hit again heavily and plunged into the sea but the two following Swordfish were unable to see whether Esmonde had succeeded in releasing his torpedo before crashing.

Swordfish W.5983, having survived the first fighter attack, was attacked by fighters again as it reached the destroyer and E-boat screen. The air gunner was killed and Sub-Lieutenant Rose severely wounded with a shot in his back. Although weak from loss of blood, he managed to hold his aircraft on a steady course towards the second big ship in the line, the *Gneisenau*. He had reached a position about 2,000 yards from the *Gneisenau* when the Swordfish's petrol tank was hit and burst open by a cannon shell from a fighter. The engine began to falter and Rose dropped his torpedo. As he turned the Swordfish, the torpedo was seen to be running a straight course, but it is known that it did not achieve a hit. Rose managed to lift his damaged aircraft over the screen again, but it crashed into the sea about 500 yards beyond. Before it sank, Sub-Lieutenant Lee, who was unwounded, managed to drag Rose out of the cockpit and into the rubber dinghy, and they were found about an hour and a half later by a British motor torpedo boat.

The third Swordfish, W.5907, was also attacked by fighters as it passed over the screen, and severely damaged and set on fire by a burst of cannon fire which wounded both Kingsmill, the pilot, and his observer, Sub-Lieutenant Samples. But the pilot managed to keep the machine flying and the rear-gunner drove off yet another fighter attack, shooting down one of them. Kingsmill dropped his torpedo at a range of less than 3,000 yards and, with great difficulty because of the damage to his aircraft and the fire, managed to turn the Swordfish in the direction of home. He tried to land his crippled aircraft on the sea near a group of small vessels but they turned out to be German E-boats and opened a heavy fire on him. He continued over them until, two or three minutes later, his engine cut out and the Swordfish crashed. As it happened the Dover motor torpedo boats, which were retiring after their torpedo attack on the enemy, saw the crash and quickly rescued the crew.

Of the attack by the second sub-flight, little is known. All three Swordfish were seen crossing the screen by Rose as he was bringing his aircraft out after his own attack. At that time they were taking violent evasive action to escape the enemy fighters but nonetheless were making towards the three enemy ships, and when last seen were within 4,000 yards of them. None of the three was seen again and there were no survivors to report the outcome of their attacks.

Reports from the German ships of this attack are confused. According to that of the *Scharnhorst*, she was attacked by four Swordfish flying very low which came in on her port quarter, three of which were shot down by fighters and the fourth by the *Scharnhorst's* anti-aircraft guns. The report mentions only one torpedo dropped, which exploded on contact with the water. The *Prinz Eugen* also reported being attacked by four aircraft at the same time and claimed to have shot down three of them. But whatever their fate, it is certain that no torpedo fired by any of the Swordfish scored a hit.

There remained the three motor torpedo boats from Ramsgate, which had sailed at the same time as those from Dover but, having a greater distance to go, had to make their attack further to the eastward. A good deal of engine trouble was experienced on the way, and with the weather closing in, reducing visibility and throwing up a confused sea, none of them was able to sight the three big German ships. MTB 32 did in fact make contact with the E-boat and destroyer screen to the northward of the *Scharnhorst, Gneisenau,* and *Prinz Eugen,* but was unable to penetrate it and could not see through the murk any sign of her target. Quite unable to accomplish anything, the three motor torpedo boats withdrew.

This was the end of the first phase of the attack on the German ships. It had unhappily achieved no tangible result in spite of the gallantry which had gone into the individual attacks by motor torpedo boats and Swordfish. It had never been expected that any of the three ships could have been sunk by these attacks even if they had succeeded in scoring hits with their torpedoes, but it had been hoped that one or two hits would have had the effect of slowing them up to gain additional time in which to mount more severe attacks. There was still the memory of how, in May 1941, a torpedo from a naval Swordfish had crippled the giant battleship *Bismarck* and held her stationary until the Home Fleet could reach her the following morning and send her to the bottom. Had a similar fate been suffered by the *Scharnhorst* or *Gneisenau* or even the *Prinz Eugen,* the gallantry and sacrifice would have been worthwhile. But this time the odds were too heavily stacked on the side of the German ships with their destroyer, torpedo boat, and E-boat screen and their massive shore-based fighter cover.

It was now the turn of the torpedo-carrying Beauforts of Coastal Command to make their attempt to stop the enemy. Nearest to the German ships was No 217 Squadron based at Thorney Island, but three aircraft of this squadron were at St Eval in Cornwall and of the seven at Thorney Island only four were at operational readiness. They were ordered to fly to Manston to rendezvous with a fighter escort and took off from Thorney Island at 13.40 hrs but got separated on the way, reaching Manston in ones and twos. Their pilots had not been briefed before leaving Thorney Island, did not know the meaning of codeword *Fuller,* and had not been informed what they were to attack, or where. It had been planned to pass them their orders in flight, but attempts to contact them by W/T failed, it not being realised at Thorney Island that they had all recently been converted from W/T to R/T.

Eventually, after circling Manston for some time, the leader landed, learned who was the enemy and his position, and took off again. He was unable for some reason to link up with his other three aircraft, but with one of them in company, set off for the Channel. The other two, after continuing to circle Manston for some time, decided to follow the general direction of other aircraft proceeding to the scene. The four made a series of unco-ordinated attacks, the first at about 15.40 hrs, but by that time the visibility was so bad and the defence, both by the escorting fighters and the anti-aircraft fire of the screen and the capital ships so intense that it was not possible to achieve more than a rough degree of accuracy. The remaining Beauforts of No 217 Squadron at Thorney Island were brought to operational readiness later in the afternoon and set off independently for the enemy. One was shot down by a German fighter on approaching the scene before it could fire its torpedo; the other two got in attacks but neither was successful.

The next Beauforts to attack were those of No 42 Squadron based at Leuchars, in Fife. They had been ordered south on February 8th but had delayed their departure because of bad weather in eastern England. Of the fourteen aircraft available only nine had torpedoes. They were therefore ordered to land at the Coastal Command station at North Coates in Norfolk to complete with torpedoes before flying on to Manston to pick up a fighter escort. Snow had fallen in East Anglia during the night and unfortunately the runway at North Coates had not been cleared. The Beauforts were diverted to the nearby fighter station at

Coltishall, where the runways had been cleared, and attempts made to bring the torpedoes by lorry from North Coates. But this operation was taking so long and with the time available for attack slipping away, it was decided not to delay the nine aircraft which had their torpedoes any longer. They took off for Manston, picked up their fighter escort, and together with five Hudson bombers, set course for the enemy, leaving Manston at about 15.30 hrs. None of the pilots had been briefed as to what the enemy was; all they had been told was that they were to attack a convoy. They were over the target area at about 16.00 hrs, just after the destroyers from Harwich had made their attacks on the three German ships and were withdrawing. Seven of the Beauforts attacked with their torpedoes, three of them unfortunately mistaking the British destroyers for German battle-cruisers but fortunately missing. Some of the Hudsons got in bombing attacks. The two remaining Beauforts failed to locate the enemy and returned with their torpedoes. No hits were made, either by the Beauforts or the Hudsons.

The last of the Coastal Command Beauforts to attempt to stop the race homewards of the three German ships were twelve of No 86 Squadron from St Eval. They were ordered to fly first to Thorney Island, which they reached at 14.30 hrs, and from there to Coltishall in Norfolk to rendezvous with a fighter escort. Coltishall was reached at 16.40 hrs but no fighters made their appearance, and so the squadron leader in command decided to set off without escort. But by this time the daylight was fast fading and in the growing dusk the Beauforts were all unable to sight the enemy. Two of them were shot down by enemy fighters; the remainder returned unscathed.

Of all the weapons which it had been planned to deploy against the Brest ships if they should attempt the Channel passage, most reliance and hope had been pinned on the Beauforts. They were modern aircraft, relatively fast for their role of torpedo-bomber, with pilots trained in this method of attack against ships. It had been unfortunate that the wide dispersal over Britain had made a co-ordinated attack impossible, unfortunate that the Leuchars squadron had been unable to come south when ordered on February

8th, and unfortunate that undue secrecy, combined with the breakdown of communications in flight, had meant that many of the pilots were not briefed as to who was the enemy and where he was. That so many of the pilots did in fact find the German ships in these conditions was remarkable. Their attacks were pressed home with great gallantry in the face of mounting difficulties, for by the time they were coming in to launch their attacks the weather had broken badly. Heavy and low cloud had taken much of the light out of the February day and the approaching dusk made even greater inroads into the visibility. The problem of ship recognition from the air, always difficult, was made even more so on this occasion by the rapidly deteriorating weather. Taking the Coastal Command attempts to stop the enemy in summary, 28 Beauforts, accompanied by some Hudsons and Beaufighters, had been deployed; fifteen Beauforts made contact with the enemy and ten dropped torpedoes aimed at the German ships and three at the British destroyers by mistake. Three Beauforts were lost. At the time three or four hits on the enemy were claimed but in fact all the torpedoes fired missed their targets.

It is time now to record the efforts of Fighter Command in this overall attempt by the Royal Navy and the Royal Air Force to stop the flying enemy. On some occasions the planned fighter cover failed to make contact with the forces they were due to escort, a state of affairs easy enough to understand in view of the short time available after the first sighting and identification of the enemy in the Channel at 11.25 hrs and the speed with which these arrangements had to be made. On the occasions when this occurred, the fighter escorts, finding their attacking forces already on the way without them, made their own way to the scene of action to do what they could to disrupt the enemy's fighter defences. In all, 398 fighters were engaged in this operation, of which seventeen were shot down, and they destroyed sixteen of the enemy.

So far, all had gone superbly well with the German plan. Fortune had smiled upon them, chiefly through the boldness of their decision to pass through the narrows of the English Channel in daylight instead of, as the British defence forces had expected, during the hours of darkness. This initial decision and its execution had caught the defence on the wrong foot, a state of affairs which was accentuated by the long start they had achieved up Channel before they were at last identified south-west of Boulogne. They had been remarkably fortunate in getting through the westernmost night air patrols without discovery, and their fortune still held good through the period after they were first located and before they were identified. Nor had it deserted them throughout the motor torpedo boat and Swordfish attacks between Calais and Dunkirk and the succeeding Coastal Command attacks with Beauforts, the deterioration in the weather coming to their assistance. They had one more extreme piece of good fortune when, at about 13.30 hrs, they passed through an undiscovered minefield, laid the previous month by HMS *Plover,* without striking one.

There was a slight setback to their remarkable run of good fortune when, at 14.32 hrs, a mine laid some days previously by Bomber Command exploded under the *Scharnhorst.* She was brought temporarily to a stop, and in accordance with the orders laid down the *Gneisenau* and *Prinz Eugen* passed her, continuing their passage at 27 knots. Vice-Admiral Ciliax signalled the destroyer *Z.29* to come alongside, and with his staff transferred to her so that he could continue to exercise command of the operation. But there was not a great deal of structural damage in the *Scharnhorst* and seventeen minutes later she was under way again and working up to 25 knots. One turret was temporarily put out of action by the explosion, but the fighting efficiency of the ship was not greatly impaired. By 15.00 hrs she was abeam of Walcheren Island, off the mouth of the River Maas, nearly two-thirds of the way home, and not all that far astern of the other ships of the squadron. Every minute that elapsed now took her, and them, further away from the danger area and the chances of further attack.

It was at this stage of the operation that control of the naval attack passed from the Flag Officer, Dover (Vice-Admiral Ramsay) to the Commander-in-Chief, Nore (Admiral Sir George d'Oyley-Lyon). The German squadron was now well beyond the limits of the Dover Command area and inside those of the Nore Command, and moreover, the only ships still to be actively engaged were destroyers belonging to that command. Vice-Admiral Ramsay suggested the transfer of naval control to the Nore at 14.11 hrs, and the Admiralty readily agreed.

There still remained two strings to the British bow, and both were on their way. From Harwich were coming six destroyers of the 16th and 21st Flotillas, and in the air were 242 aircraft of Bomber Command, due to attack in three waves.

The six destroyers concerned were the *Campbell, Vivacious* and *Worcester,* of the 21st Destroyer Flotilla, and the *Mackay, Whitshed* and *Walpole,* of the 16th Flotilla. The senior officer (Captain D.21) was Captain C. T. M. Pizey and he took operational command of all six. All of them were elderly vessels of World War I vintage whose task in this war was the protection of East Coast convoys. They were fortunately all at sea exercising off the coast of Suffolk and so required no period of notice to come to instant readiness, and they were on their way as soon as the signal from Dover stating that the German squadron was coming up Channel was received in the *Campbell* at 11.56 hrs. Their original plan was to attack the enemy ships in the vicinity of the West Hinder Buoy off the Belgian coast, passing through the swept channel in the southern extremity of the East Coast mine barrier. This was still possible on the assumption that the speed of advance of the enemy was 20 knots, but as soon as Captain Pizey worked out from his plot that the enemy's speed was 27 knots, he realised that he would have to make his attack much further to the eastward. He was receiving the broadcasts from Dover of the enemy's position as indicated by the radar plot made every few minutes, and it was this that revealed the speed of the German squadron. His only hope of interception now was to abandon the swept channel approach and cross the minefield direct, to make contact with the enemy off the mouth of the River Maas. At 13.18 hrs he made the signal to his destroyers to alter course due east and increase speed to 28 knots, a course taking them direct across the mine barrier. Captain Pizey estimated that this new course would bring him into contact with the enemy at about 15.30 hrs.

Just as the destroyers were crossing the edge of the minefield the main bearings of HMS *Walpole* began to run and she had no other course but to turn round and proceed at reduced speed to harbour. The remaining five continued eastward at 28 knots and by 14.30 hrs were clear across the mine barrier.

They had been bombed spasmodically as they crossed the minefield, but with little accuracy, and the only attack which fell close, some 30 yards from HMS *Worcester,* came from a British bomber at 14.45 hrs. There was fortunately no damage to the ship. But in the operations room at the Nore headquarters some anxiety was being felt as the afternoon wore on with no sighting reports of the enemy even though shadowing aircraft were believed to be in combat. It was thought, according to the plot, that Captain Pizey's destroyers might be too far to the north and east, and at 15.09 hrs a signal was despatched to him that if he had not made contact by 15.15 hrs, he was to search to the south-west. It was received on the bridge of the *Campbell* at 15.17 hrs, but almost at that exact moment the *Campbell's* Type 271 radar produced two large echoes, bearing 145° and distant nine and a half miles. Two minutes later a third echo was recorded. The first two were the *Gneisenau* and *Prinz Eugen,* the third was the *Scharnhorst,* catching up after her short stop when she had exploded the mine.

As yet no ships were visible, as the low cloud in the area and the approaching twilight had reduced the earlier visibility of about seven miles to four or less, and it was continuing to close in. The radar plot showed Captain Pizey that with the enemy's speed still in the neighbourhood of 27-28 knots, he had little chance of gaining bearing and that his most promising line of attack was to close the enemy as fast as possible until he sighted the ships, and then to turn towards them on an attacking course, pressing in as close as possible before firing. The actual moment of firing would depend on the strength of the opposition, for it was essential to get the torpedoes away before the destroyers suffered such damage as to make them unmanageable.

His present course of 075° was about ideal for closing, and

before long large numbers of aircraft were encountered, both German and British, flying in and out of the cloud. An oddity of the action at this stage was that many of the German aircraft considered Captain Pizey's destroyers as friendly, firing their recognition signals of four red balls in diamond shape so that they should not be fired at, while most of the British aircraft obviously considered the destroyers as enemy vessels to be bombed and attacked by cannon fire. On some occasions the destroyers opened fire on aircraft which later they recognised as friendly but none, either German or British, were shot down.

In the midst of all this air confusion, gun flashes were sighted to the southward from the *Campbell's* bridge at 15.42 hrs, bearing 155°, followed by anti-aircraft tracer fire. A minute later two large ships were seen in line ahead about five cables apart, with a close screen of destroyers disposed on their port bow. They were the *Gneisenau* and *Prinz Eugen.* The *Scharnhorst* was not visible, still being astern of the other two after her involuntary stop. The distance was four miles, just about the limit of existing visibility.

The destroyers, until now in line ahead, turned to attack in two divisions, the first consisting of the *Campbell, Vivacious* and *Worcester,* the second of the *Mackay* and *Whitshed.* They went in on a slight but continuous zig-zag to throw off the enemy's gunfire, not only from the German destroyer screen but also from the bigger ships engaging with main armament. Simultaneously they were being attacked by aircraft, at which they fired continuously with all available close range weapons. In his Report of Proceedings, Captain Pizey wrote: "It is no exaggeration to say that every twenty seconds one or more enemy aircraft appeared out of the clouds." Hits were observed on some of the aircraft though none was seen to fall into the sea.

The three destroyers of the first division were frequently straddled by the main armament of the *Gneisenau* and *Prinz Eugen* but miraculously none of them was hit. They were closing fast now and the time was very near when Captain Pizey must turn to fire torpedoes if the destroyers were to get them away before being crippled. His mind was made up for him when, at 15.47 hrs, an 11in shell landed just short of the

Campbell, failed to explode or ricochet and "dived under the ship like a porpoise". The good fortune which had brought them so far without being hit and disabled could not be expected to last much longer and at 15.47½ hrs the *Campbell* turned and fired. The *Vivacious,* on the *Campbell's* starboard quarter, turned and fired at the same time, both ships taking as their target the leading battle-cruiser. The *Campbell,* after her turn, retired to the north-east to engage the enemy destroyers, the *Vivacious* to the north-west.

Lt-Commander Coates, commanding the *Worcester,* third ship in the division, apparently did not see the *Campbell's* firing turn and pressed on towards the enemy. She now came under the concentrated fire of both the big ships and the German destroyers, but was not hit until 15.50 hrs, by which time she had closed the range to 2,400 yards. It was a very heavy hit and all her bridge communications were severed. As a result all her torpedoes had to be fired in local control and ran harmlessly parallel to the enemy's course. Almost immediately she was hit again by two shells in Nos 1 and 2 boiler rooms and was brought to a stop. She lay beam on to the enemy, a stationary target for the concentrated fire of every German ship, large and small, within range. She was hit repeatedly for the next ten minutes until gradually the German squadron moved out of range.

The two destroyers of the second division, which turned for their run in towards the enemy at the same time as the *Campbell,* and were therefore more to the west, did not sight the leading battle-cruiser and saw only the rear ship indistinctly. But at 15.42 hrs a large ship was seen bearing 150° which Captain Wright, in the *Mackay,* assumed to be a battle-cruiser. She was in fact the *Prinz Eugen,* swinging north while taking evasive action to avoid a torpedo fired by one of the Beauforts of 217 Squadron. As she altered course back towards the *Gneisenau* the *Mackay* turned to starboard and fired at 15.46½ hrs, but the *Prinz Eugen* again took evading action by making a 16-point turn right round to the southward, causing the torpedoes to miss ahead. The *Whitshed* continued in and turned to fire at 15.49 hrs, but also missed.

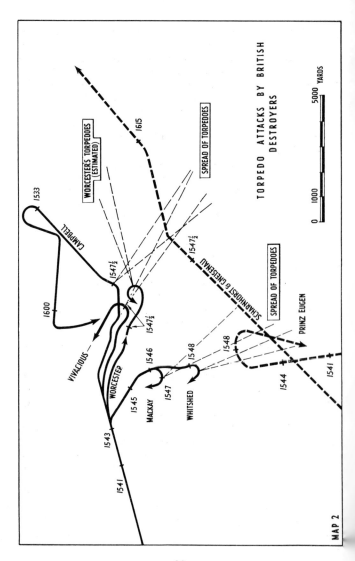

TORPEDO ATTACKS BY BRITISH
DESTROYERS

WORCESTER'S TORPEDOES
(ESTIMATED)

SPREAD OF TORPEDOES

SPREAD OF TORPEDOES

PRINZ EUGEN

SCHARNHORST & GNEISENAU

CAMPBELL

VIVACIOUS

WORCESTER

MACKAY

WHITSHED

1533

1600

1547½

1547½

1547½

1546

1547

1545

1548

1548

1544

1541

1543

1541

1541

1615

0   1000   5000   YARDS

MAP 2

68

By the time these destroyer attacks were made the weather had deteriorated considerably. The wind had strengthened to the extent where it was kicking up a sea so rough that it was breaking green over the bows and stern of the destroyers, with spray flying continuously over the bridges. Water was at times knee deep on deck, and the ships rolled so heavily, particularly the second division which was beam-on to the sea during the approach, that it was extremely difficult to train the torpedo tubes. In conditions such as these, and in ships of an age where loading and training of guns and tubes was all by hand, the difficulties facing the gun and torpedo crews was considerable.

The *Worcester,* during the ten minutes or so she lay stopped and broadside-on to the German ships, was very heavily hit. She was holed in several places, including No 1 and No 2 boiler rooms and the fore peak, her mast and galley funnel were shot away and the bridge superstructure riddled with shot holes, her wireless office was wrecked, and a great amount of internal damage caused by explosions. Further damage was caused by the considerable flooding which inevitably followed the holing of her hull.

As the German ships moved away eastward on their homeward course the *Worcester* wallowed badly in the rising sea, her heavy rolling made more violent by the large amount of sea water in her internal spaces, which also had the effect of making the rolling more sluggish with a consequent added danger of capsizing. In these circumstances Lt-Commander Coates gave the order "Prepare to abandon ship", which in the noise and confusion was passed down to the upper deck as "Abandon ship'. The liferafts and Carley floats were launched and many of the wounded placed in them before the order was countermanded, and with the ship drifting away down to leeward, many of the rafts and floats could not be brought back alongside. One of them capsized and its occupants were being dragged out of the water when two destroyers were sighted on an approach course.

It was thought at first on board the *Worcester* that these were German destroyers from the *Gneisenau's* screen coming back to finish off the stricken ship but they were soon recognised as the *Campbell* and *Vivacious*. Both sighted the Carley floats in the water and stopped alongside them to bring the occupants on board. This task was made even more difficult by the increasing roughness of the sea, the inability of the men, wounded and suffering from cold, to help themselves, and the constant attack by aircraft, which were however kept at bay by anti-aircraft fire from the ships. But at 16.15 hrs three Beauforts, coming in low over the sea, dropped their torpedoes with an accuracy which forced HMS *Campbell* to go full speed astern to avoid being hit. The wash from her propellers capsized some of the rafts and floats which were lying alongside, throwing their occupants into the bitterly cold water.

By an hour later all the men in the water and from the rafts had been rescued and the *Campbell* closed the *Worcester* to take her in tow. But by this time, the *Worcester* had raised a sufficient head of steam to go ahead at six knots and Lt-Commander Coates informed Captain Pizey that he was confident of being able to reach Harwich without assistance. As a signal from the C-in-C Nore was also received at this time ordering all destroyers which had fired torpedoes to return to Harwich to reload for a second attack on the enemy, the *Campbell* passed the compass course to steer for Harwich to the *Worcester* and made her own way back, accompanied by the *Vivacious,* at full speed.

Meanwhile the *Worcester* made the best of her way home, making good a speed of about six knots. Twice during the night she lost steam through loss of feed water, and on one of these occasions, when rolling very heavily beam on to the sea, she was forced to jettison all gear high up, including the rangefinder, to provide additional stability. Eventually, after a very difficult passage, she reached the Sunk Light, off Harwich at dawn on the 13th and steamed slowly into harbour.

Following the original plan drawn up by the Air Ministry (see Chapter 1) the bombers engaged in the operation were to be armed with 500lb SAP (armour-piercing) bombs, but in the actual event this was not practicable as the low cloud precluded these aircraft from attacking at high level, an essential requirement if armour-piercing bombs were to be effective. They were therefore armed with high-explosive bombs. A total of 242 aircraft were despatched by Bomber Command in three waves, attacking between 14.45 hrs and 17.00 hrs. Few, if any, of the pilots had been trained in attacking a moving target, and in any case the cloud density (10/10ths at 1,500ft) made conditions doubly difficult. Of the 242 aircraft despatched, only 39 found the enemy and dropped their bombs. No hits were obtained but two of the smaller escorts, the torpedo boats *T.13* and *Jaguar,* were slightly damaged by splinters and left the escort to put into Rotterdam. They were accompanied by the destroyer *Friedrich Ihn* which had developed boiler trouble.

There remained now but one final shot in the British locker. A request was made to Bomber Command by the Admiralty for magnetic mines to be laid in the Elbe estuary, the approach waters to the Kiel Canal. Twenty aircraft took off at 23.00 hrs, of which twelve laid mines, but none of the German ships passed near them.

Yet the two battle-cruisers were not to reach home entirely unscathed. After the British destroyers' torpedo attacks, the German ships had separated further, the *Gneisenau* and *Prinz Eugen* continuing at 27 knots, the *Scharnhorst* reducing to 21 knots, possibly an aftermath of the mine damage she had received earlier. At 19.55 hrs, when north of Vlieland, the *Gneisenau* was brought to a stop when a magnetic mine exploded under her bottom. It was one which had been laid by aircraft several days earlier. The damage, however, was relatively slight and after a few minutes she was able to proceed again, working up to 25 knots. She and the *Prinz Eugen* reached Brunsbuttel, the western entrance to the Kiel Canal, at 07.00 hrs on the 13th.

The *Scharnhorst,* too, was not yet safely home. Like the *Gneisenau* she passed over a magnetic mine, similarly laid some days earlier, at 21.34 hrs. In her case the damage was much more serious and she came to a stop. Her port engine was put out of action, both steering motors were damaged, her turret training gear, fire control system and echo-sounding apparatus broke down, and she shipped 1,000 tons of water. It was 50 minutes before her engine room department could get the centre and starboard engines working again and the *Scharnhorst* was able to proceed at twelve knots. She made her way slowly to Wilhelmshafen where she secured alongside at about 10.30 hrs on the 13th.

From the German point of view, Operation *Cerberus* had been successfully concluded; from the British, Operation *Fuller* had failed.

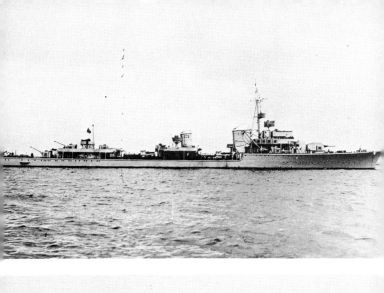

Top: A German Z-class destroyer.
Above: The German destroyer *Friedrich Ihn*.

Top: The *Scharnhorst, Gneisenau* and *Prinz Eugen,* with their close escort, photographed during their passage up Channel in February 1942.
Above: The British flotilla leader HMS *Campbell* which led the destroyer attack on the German squadron.

Top: A German torpedo boat of the Falke class.
Above: The German destroyer *Richard Beitzen*.

The German battlecruiser
Scharnhorst.

The German battlecruiser
Gneisenau. The photograph
shows her with her original
straight stem, later replaced
with a flared bow.

Above left: Camouflage netting spread over the cruiser *Prinz Eugen* while in dry-dock at Brest.
Left: A photograph taken on board the *Prinz Eugen* during her escape up Channel. Her port AA guns have just been fired.
Top: A German Heinkel He 111. This particular aircraft was captured by the British and is seen with RAF markings.
Above: A German T-class torpedo boat.

Above: A torpedo being loaded into the tube of a British motor torpedo boat.
Left: Captain C. T. M. (later Admiral Sir Mark) Pizey who led the destroyer attack in HMS *Campbell* on the German squadron during their passage up Channel.

CHAPTER FOUR

Aftermath

Vice-Admiral Ciliax was justly pleased with the success of
the operation as a whole, particularly in view of the recent
disaster off the coast of Malaya when the *Prince of Wales*
and *Repulse* had been sunk by shore-based Japanese
bombers and torpedo-bombers. Their vulnerability to air
attack had not augured well for the safety of the Brest
squadron in somewhat similar circumstances, even though,
unlike the British ships, it would have continuous fighter
cover. Its immunity from disaster lay equally, perhaps,
between its fighter cover, the deterioration in the weather
during the periods of attack, and a lack of training both in
torpedo-bombing and in the bombing of moving targets.

Yet not all the reaction in Germany was euphoric.
Commenting on the operation a few days later, the Naval
War Diary reported: "A deep impression has been made on
British public opinion. That it was possible for a group of
enemy battleships to sail up the Channel in broad daylight
without being stopped by the Royal Navy or Royal Air Force
was a serious blow to faith in British mastery of the sea and
air, and above all in the co-operation between the two
Services.

"At the same time the unfavourable effect of withdrawal
from Brest on our strategic position in the North Atlantic
began to make itself felt. Within a few days we received news
that the British battleships had been withdrawn from the
North Atlantic convoy service and were assembled in the
north of Scotland.

"And Prime Minister Churchill announced in the House
of Commons—and this was not only propaganda—that the
departure of the German ships from the Atlantic coast had

73

relieved the Admiralty of an incubus which had been threatening them for months".

Admiral Raeder held the same opinion and expressed it more briefly and succinctly. "We have won a tactical victory", he wrote, "and suffered a strategic defeat".

The reaction in Britain was violently critical. In a leading article, *The Times* expressed the public feeling when it wrote: "Vice-Admiral Ciliax has succeeded where the Duke of Medina Sidonia failed. Nothing more mortifying to the pride of our sea power has happened since the seventeenth century". In face of opinion such as this, and as a result of serious disquiet in the House of Commons, the Government set up an independent Board of Inquiry into the handling of the operation. It was presided over by Mr Justice Bucknill and its other members were Admiral Sir Hugh Binney and Air Marshal Sir Edgar Ludlow-Hewitt. The Board sat for twelve days and produced its report in March. On March 18th the deputy Prime Minister, Mr Clement Attlee, reported to the House of Commons that the report had been received and studied, but could not be made public as it contained information of value to the enemy. He also reported that the general findings of the Board did not reveal "any serious deficiencies in either foresight, co-operation, or organisation between the Services concerned and their respective commands".

Vice-Admiral Ramsay's Report of Proceedings was critical of the failure to detect the enemy either by the night patrols or by the early "Jim Crow" reconnaissances, though he also blamed himself for his own failure to make a more accurate estimate of the time the German squadron would arrive in the Straits of Dover. Had his headquarters been informed at the time of the three-hour gap in the "Stopper" patrol, the failure of the "Line SE" patrol, and the curtailment of the "Habo" patrol, it might well have alerted his command to the fact that the German ships could be well on their way up Channel. That no reports of failure in the three patrols had been made to Dover produced the impression there that they had been fully flown as usual, and if they had, then the Brest squadron had not yet departed. Admiral Ramsay was equally critical of the failure of the dawn "Jim

Crow" patrol to sight the squadron. "Had they been sighted then", he wrote, "there would have been ample time for our main striking forces to get off and make attacks in the narrow waters of Dover Straits. We would have had maximum advantage, and would have been able to use our numerical and tactical air superiority, combined with accurate knowledge of the enemy's path on the radar plot. Failing other information during the night, a successful dawn reconnaissance to the westward of Dover Command would have given two hours' extra warning of their approach".

The report of the Bucknill Board of Inquiry was made public after the war and was presented to Parliament as a White Paper in March 1946. It was divided into two parts, a narrative of events and an examination of certain important questions arising from those events. It found that "co-ordination (between commands) was not entirely successful. For example, in the provision of escorts for the Swordfish", though the "later co-operation between the commands (of the Royal Air Force) seems to have been complete". It was critical of the failure to fly a reconnaissance to the westward after the known breakdown of the night patrols, suggesting that Coastal Command, had it feared for the safety of its aircraft flying such patrols in daylight, should have requested fighter escort from Fighter Command.

On one of the key points in the delay after the initial sighting of getting the information through, the failure of the "Jim Crow" pilots to break R/T silence and report their sightings over the air, the Board found that no blame could be attached to them. This was, perhaps, the most surprising of its findings, as the original Fighter Command order required R/T silence only on the outward journey and also gave a discretionary permission to break it in an emergency. More surprising still was their concurrence in Group Captain Beamish's action in maintaining R/T silence, as he had recognised the ships themselves when he flew over them and should surely have considered that fact as an emergency which warranted the breaking of R/T silence, as the specific order allowed. One of the results of this experience of February 12 was a new Fighter Command order making it obligatory to report at once the sighting of any enemy ship of destroyer size or larger.

The Bucknill report was also critical in a slightly back-handed way of the state of training of the Beaufort torpedo-bombers. "There is no doubt", it stated, "that the well-timed delivery of synchronised attacks by torpedo-bombers is an operation which demands a very high standard of training and efficiency, a standard which the Board realises is difficult to attain in time of war. The Board ventures to express the view that against fast, heavily armoured ships the most effective air weapon available at present is undoubtedly the torpedo-bomber. The need for the development of a powerful and highly trained striking force of torpedo-bombers seems to be one which calls for urgent consideration".

The Bucknill Board of Inquiry made no mention or criticism of the Admiralty's failure to intervene with ships of the Home Fleet at Scapa Flow. It was, of course, quite impossible for capital ships based at Scapa Flow to reach the scene of action in the time available after the first sighting of the German ships; if they had sailed at once when the first report was received, they could not have been within 200 miles of the German squadron when the latter were reaching the German coastal waters. There was, however, a considerable public belief that part of the Home Fleet should have been moved south, perhaps to the Humber, when the German move was thought to be imminent. Had this been done, and the ships kept at immediate notice, it would have been possible to make contact with the enemy in the winter darkness in the vicinity of Heligoland with the possible prospect of a night action. But to do so would have meant abandoning one or both of the prior commitments with which the Home Fleet was charged, which were capital ship escort of the WS troop convoys and the denial to the *Tirpitz* of a clear route into the Atlantic and the main convoy routes. To bring a squadron of the Home Fleet, powerful enough to match the *Scharnhorst, Gneisenau* and *Prinz Eugen,* south to the Humber to await the passage of the Brest squadron up the Channel would in fact have meant the abandonment of both priorities, since the strength of the fleet in Scapa at the time had been reduced, because of its current commitments, to one modern battleship, the *King George V,* one older battleship, the *Rodney,* and one even older battle-cruiser, the *Renown.* In fact the *Renown* was at the time in the Clyde to provide capital ship escort for the WS convoy which was on the point of sailing to the Middle East.

It was for all these reasons that from the start it was realised that the operation must basically be an air operation, with the Royal Navy contributing what light forces were available within striking distance of the enemy. All the initial planning had been done on that basis, and given the efficient functioning of the early warning patrols, might well have achieved the desired success of disabling the ships in the narrows of the Dover Straits where they would have been within range of the British coastal batteries.

In its final summing up of the operation the Bucknill Board of Inquiry stated: "Apart from the weakness of our forces, the main reason for our failure to do more damage to the enemy was the fact that his presence was not detected earlier, and this was due to a breakdown of night patrols and the omission to send out strong morning reconnaissance. All operational orders said they would pass through in darkness". This in fact is not quite the case as the original Air Ministry directive to the three commands, Coastal, Bomber and Fighter, did allow for the fact that the ships might not go through the narrows in darkness and called for planning for daylight attacks which, in the opinion of the Air Ministry, would offer "a unique opportunity" to mount attacks "to the maximum practicable effort". That these attacks did not develop as planned was due, in some respects at least, to the fact that none of the forces actually engaged, naval as well as air, were fully geared to combat the element of last-minute surprise. Perhaps too much reliance had been placed on the early morning patrols to locate the enemy ships at the outset of their break-out and not sufficient allowance made for the frailties of aircrews and equipment.

That such tremendous surprise had been achieved by the Brest squadron in their break-out — they had covered some 270 miles of their 550-mile passage before discovery — was a cause of considerable public alarm that so powerful an enemy force could steam through waters so close to Britain for so long a time immune from detection. For most of this passage they had been, of course, beyond the range of shore-based radar, though for the last two hours of their passage before actual recognition they had appeared on the British radar plots, though not identified. It did not argue well, in the public estimation, for the degree of alertness on the part of British forces in the midst of war. But the element of surprise, particularly in naval warfare where the areas of sea are so vast, lies almost entirely in the hands of the force which initiates the action. Vice-Admiral Ciliax, in complete secrecy so far as the British were concerned, could choose the date for the operation, the time of departure, the route to be taken, and the degree of radio-countermeasures to be adopted to disguise the operation in the form of wireless routines and radar jamming. The British forces had to guess at all these vital things, and had to guess also at the varying degrees of readiness required by their forces in relation to all necessary maintenance routines of ships and aircraft. The British guess, which was based largely on the belief that Vice-Admiral Ciliax would naturally choose to pass through the area of maximum danger to himself at the time most favourable to his ships, was wrong by about five hours, and by that amount added to the degree of surprise that Vice-Admiral Ciliax was able to achieve. He was also greatly aided by the failure of the night early-warning patrols which, had they operated efficiently during their prescribed times of flight, would have picked up and identified the Brest squadron probably before midnight on February 11th. With that degree of warning there could well have been a very different result to this bold operation.

It remains only to record the ultimate fate of the three major ships concerned. The *Gneisenau*, after passing through the Kiel Canal on February 13th, was placed in dry-dock at Kiel for the repair of her mine damage and the replacement, which had been long pre-planned, of her 11in guns by a 16in armament. She was caught there on the nights of February 25th, 26th, and 27th by British bombers in three successive raids by 61, 49, and 68 aircraft respectively and severely damaged, her forecastle being wrecked and her back broken. She was eventually towed to Gdynia where she was grounded to act as a harbour defence blockship. The *Prinz Eugen* was the only one of the three ships which was able at once to fulfil Hitler's desire to reinforce the naval forces in northern Norway to counter the invasion by Britain which he thought to be imminent. On February 21st, flying the flag of Vice-Admiral Ciliax, she sailed in company with the *Admiral Scheer* from Bruns-buttel to join the *Tirpitz* in Aasfjord, near Trondheim. She was sighted by British reconnaissance aircraft during the night of February 22nd in Grinstad Fjord, south of Bergen, and at 06.00 hrs on the 23rd was torpedoed by the British submarine *Trident* but not damaged as seriously as had been hoped and managed to reach Aasfjord later that day. She returned to Kiel for repairs and later served as flagship of the Baltic Fleet. She made two more attempts to reach Norway early in 1943 accompanied by the *Scharnhorst* but on each occasion was sighted by reconnaissance aircraft off the Skaw and turned back. She was still in the Baltic at the end of the war and was allocated to the United States on the division of the German fleet. Her final end came at Bikini Atoll in 1947 when she was used as a trial ship in the explosion of the first hydrogen bomb.

The *Scharnhorst* finally reached Norway in February 1943 and was sighted in Altenfjord with the *Tirpitz* and the heavy cruiser *Admiral Hipper* on the 11th. She and the *Tirpitz* appeared off the island of Spitzbergen on September 6th, 1943, and bombarded the British wireless installations there. On September 22nd she was fortunate to be away from her moorings on exercises when the British midget submarines arrived in Altenfjord and damaged the *Tirpitz* with their charges. Towards the end of the year Admiral Dönitz, who had succeeded Admiral Raeder in supreme command of the German navy, decided to use the *Scharnhorst* in a surface attack on a British convoy bound to North Russia. Orders for her to sail arrived at 14.00 hours on Christmas Day and, flying the flag of Rear-Admiral Bey, who had commanded the destroyer escort during the escape of the Brest squadron up Channel on February 12th, 1942, she sailed an hour or two later. Early the next morning she was sighted, engaged, and shadowed by three British cruisers which were covering the convoy. As she ran from them to the southward, unknown to her the British battleship *Duke of York,* with the cruiser *Jamaica* and four destroyers in company, was closing her from the west. In her last moments she redeemed, perhaps, some of the more sorry aspects of her earlier career, for she fought gallantly enough against tremendous odds until she was overwhelmed and sunk.

British Forces Engaged

Destroyers

Campbell	Captain C. T. M. Pizey,	
	DSO	Captain D.21
Vivacious	Lt-Cdr R. Alexander	
Worcester	Lt-Cdr E. C. Coates	
Mackay	Captain J. P. Wright,	
	DSO	Captain D.16
Whitshed	Lt-Cdr W. A. Juniper	
Walpole	Lt-Cdr J. H. Eadon	

Motor Torpedo Boats

No 221	Lt-Cdr E. N. Pumphrey,	
	DSC	Based on Dover
No 219	Temp. Sub-Lt M. Arnold-	
	Foster, RNVR	,,
No 45	Lt L. J. H. Gamble, DSC	,,
No 44	Sub-Lt R. F. Saunders,	
	DSC, RANVR	,,
No 48	Lt C. A. Law, RCNVR	,,
No 32	Lt D. J. Long	Based on Ramsgate
No 18	Sub-Lt I. C. Trelawney,	
	RNVR	,,
No 71	Sub-Lt O. B. Mabee,	
	RNVR	,,

Motor Gunboats

No 43	Lt P. F. S. Gould,	
	DSC	Based on Dover
No 41	Lt R. King	,,

FAA Swordfish

W.5984	Lt-Cdr E. Esmonde, *DSO*	825 Squadron
W.5983	Sub-Lt B. W. Rose, RNVR	,,
W. 5907	Sub-Lt C. M. Kingsmill, RNVR	,,
W. 4523	Lt J. C. Thompson	,,
W. 5985	Sub-Lt C. R. Wood	,,
W. 5978	Sub-Lt P. Bligh, RNVR	,,

German Forces Engaged

Scharnhorst	Vice-Admiral O. Ciliax	
	Kapitän zur See K. Hoffman	
Gneisenau	Kapitän zur See O. Fein	
Prinz Eugen	Kapitän zur See H. Brinkmann	
Z.25	Korvettenkapitän H. Peters	5th Destroyer Flotilla
Z.29	Korvettenkapitän Rechel	,,
Richard Beitzen	Kapitän zur See F. Berger (C.O 5th D.F.)	,,
	Korvettenkapitän von Davidson	,,
Paul Jacobi	Korvettenkapitän Schlieper	,,
Friedrich Ihn	Korvettenkapitän G. Wachsmuth	,,

Hermann Schoemann	Korvettenkapitän Wittig	,,
T.2	Kapitänleutnant Goedecke	2nd Torpedo Boat Flotilla
T.4	Kapitänleutnant Sommerlatt	,,
T.5	Kapitänleutnant Koppenhagen	,,
T.11	Kapitänleutnant Grund	,,
T.12	Kapitänleutnant Mellin	,,
T.13	Kapitänleutnant Gotzmann	3rd Torpedo Boat Flotilla
T.14	Kapitänleutnant Juttner	,,
T.15	Kapitänleutnant J. Quedenfeldt	,,
T.16	Kapitänleutnant Düvelius	,,
T.17	Kapitänleutnant Blöse	,,
Kondor	Kapitänleutnant Burkart	5th Torpedo Boat Flotilla
Falke	Kapitänleutnant Hoffman	,,
Seeadler	Kapitänleutnant Kohlauf	,,
Iltis	Kapitänleutnant Jacobsen	,,
Jaguar	Kapitänleutnant F. K. Paul	,,

British Forces — Data

Campbell
Mackay

Displacement	1,530 tons standard, 2,010 full load
Dimensions	332.5 (oa) x 31.75 x 12.25 feet
Machinery	3 Yarrow boilers, Parsons turbines, 2 shafts; 40,000SHP = 31 knots
Armament	5 x 4.7in, 1 x 3in A/A, 6 x 21in torpedo tubes in triple mountings
Complement	138

Name	Builder	Laid Down	Launched	Completed
Campbell	Cammell Laird	1917	21.9.18	21.12.18
Mackay	Cammell Laird	1917	21.12.18	6.19

Whitshed
Walpole
Vivacious
Worcester

Displacement	1,120 tons standard (*Whitshed* and *Worcester* 1,100 tons), 1,500 full load
Dimensions	312 (oa) x 29.5 x 10 feet
Machinery	3 Yarrow boilers (*Worcester,* White Forster), Brown-Curtis geared turbines, 2 shafts; 27,000SHP = 31 knots
Armament	4 x 4.7in (*Walpole* and *Vivacious* 4 x 4in Mk V), 1 x 3in A/A, 2 x 2pdr pompom; 6 x 21in torpedo tubes in triple mountings
Complement	134

Name	Builder	Laid Down	Launched	Completed
Whitshed	Swan Hunter	1918	31.1.19	11.7.19
Walpole	Doxford	1917	12.2.18	7.8.18
Vivacious	Yarrow	1917	3.11.17	12.17
Worcester	White	1918	24.10.19	20.9.22

MTB 221, 219, 45, 44, 48, 22
Armament 2 x 21in torpedoes, 2 x 0.5in guns, 2 x Lewis guns

MTB 18, 71
Armament 2 x 18in torpedoes, 4 x Vickers, 2 x Lewis guns

MGB 43, 41
Armament 2 x 0.5in guns, 1 x Oerlikon, 2 x Lewis guns

APPENDIX FOUR

German Forces — Data

Scharnhorst
Gneisenau
Displacement 31,800 tons standard, 38,900 tons full load
Dimensions 741.5 (wl), 771 (oa) x 98.5 x 32.5 feet
Machinery 12 Wagner boilers (8 at 661lb, 4 at 735lb at 868°F); 3 shafts geared Brown-Boveri turbines; 160,000SHP = 31.5 knots, 6,300 tons oil fuel; radius of action 10,500 miles at 17 knots and 8,750 miles at 19 knots
Armour Krupp Main belt, 13in amidships tapering to 5in forward and 3in aft. Decks, upper 2in, main 3.25-4.25in Turrets, main armament, 14.25in (face), 9.75in (side), 4in (rear); secondary armament, 6in. Barbettes, 14in

Armament	9 x 11in/45 cal. in triple turrets; 12 x 5in/55 cal. HA/LA in 4 double and 4 single turrets; 14 x 4.1in/65 cal. H/A in 7 double turrets; 18 x 37mm, 44 x 20mm A/A. 6 x 21in torpedo tubes in triple mountings. 4 Arado 196 seaplanes, 1 catapult
Complement	1,800

Name	Builder	Laid Down	Launched	Completed
Scharnhorst	Wilhelmshafen DY	1934	3.10.36	7.1.39
Gneisenau	Deutsche Werke	1934	6.8.36	21.5.38

Prinz Eugen

Displacement	15,700 tons standard, 18,600 tons full load
Dimensions	654.5 (oa) x 71 x 15 feet
Machinery	8 H.B. boilers; 4 shafts geared Brown-Boveri turbines, with diesels for cruising speeds; 80,000SHP = 32 knots
Armour	Krupp 5in vertical side. Bridge, 2in. Turrets, 2in
Armament	8 x 8in/55 cal. in double turrets; 12 x 4.1in/65 cal. H/A in 4 double and 4 single turrets; 12 x 37mm A/A. 12 x 21in torpedo tubes in triple mountings, 4 Arado seaplanes, 1 catapult
Complement	810

Name	Builder	Laid Down	Launched	Completed
Prinz Eugen	Germania	1936	1938	1940

Z.25, Z.29

Displacement	2,600 tons standard, 3,600 tons full load
Dimensions	416.75 (oa) x 39.25 x 15 feet
Machinery	6 Wagner boilers; 2 shafts, geared Wagner turbines; 70,000SHP = 38.5 knots
Armament	5 x 5.9in/48 cal. HA/LA in 1 double and 3 single turrets; 6 x 37mm, 8 x 20mm A/A;

8 x 21in torpedo tubes in quadruple mountings

Complement   321

Name	Builder	Laid Down	Launched	Completed
Z.25	Germania	1939	1940	1940
Z.29	A.G. Weser	1939	15.10.40	25.6.41

Richard Beitzen
Paul Jacobi
Friedrich Ihn
Hermann Schoemann

Displacement	1,625 tons standard, 2,150 full load
Dimensions	374 (oa) x 37 x 9.5 feet
Machinery	Geared turbines, 2 shafts, 45,000SHP = 31 knots
Armament	5 x 5in HA/LA in 1 double and 3 single turrets; 4 x 20mm A/A; 8 x 21in torpedo tubes in quadruple mountings
Complement	283

Name	Builder	Laid Down	Launched	Completed
Beitzen	Deutsche Werke	1935	1937	1938
Jacobi	Germania	1936	1938	1939
Ihn	Blohm & Voss	1935	1937	1938
Schoemann	Germania	1936	1938	1939

T.2, T.4, T.5, T.11, T.12, T.13, T.14, T.15, T.16, T.17

Displacement	600 tons standard, 760 full load
Dimensions	267 (oa) x 28.25 x 6.25 feet
Machinery	Geared turbines, 2 shafts, 27,000SHP = 36 knots
Armament	1 x 4.1in HA/LA, 2 x 37mm A/A, 6 x 21in torpedo tubes in triple mountings
Builders	F. Schichau, Elbing; Deschimag, Bremen
Date of Launch	End of 1938 to mid-1939
Date of Completion	1940
Complement	105

Kondor, Falke, Seeadler, Iltis, Jaguar

Displacement	800 tons standard, 1,000 deep load
Dimensions	304 (oa) x 28 x 9 feet
Machinery	Geared turbines, 2 shafts, Schulz-Thornycroft boilers; 25,000SHP = 34 knots
Armament	3 x 4.1in, 2 x 1pdr A/A, 6 x 21in torpedo tubes in triple mountings
Builder	All built at Wilhelmshafen DY
Date of Launch	Late 1927-early 1928
Date of Completion	1929-1930
Complement	123

E-boats, 3 flotillas

Armament	2 x 21in torpedoes, 2 x 20mm guns

APPENDIX FIVE

Aircraft

British

Fleet Air Arm:	6 Fairey Swordfish each armed with 1 x 1,500lb torpedo
Royal Air Force: Coastal Command	28 Beaufort torpedo bombers, each armed with 1 x 1,500lb torpedo
	7 Hudson bombers
Fighter Command	398 Spitfire, Hurricane and Whirlwind fighters
Bomber Command	242 Blenheim, Halifax, Hampden, Manchester, Stirling, and Wellington bombers

Aircraft losses

Fleet Air Arm	6 Swordfish
Coastal Command	3 Beauforts, 2 Hudsons
Fighter Command	8 Hurricanes, 5 Spitfires, 4 Whirlwinds
Bomber Command	9 Hampdens, 4 Wellingtons, 2 Blenheims

German

Night Fighters	30 Junkers 88 "night destroyers"
Day Fighters	250 Messerschmitt 109, Messerschmitt 110, Junkers 88 and Focke-Wulf 190 fighters
Bombers	Unknown number Heinkel 110, Dornier, Junkers 87 bombers

Note: As many of the German Air Force records covering this operation were destroyed at the end of the war, the above numbers are unreliable and details of losses are not known.

APPENDIX SIX

Casualties

British

Fleet Air Arm — 13 killed and missing, 3 wounded
HMS *Worcester* — 23 killed and missing, 4 died of wounds, 18 wounded

German

Prinz Eugen — 1 killed
Jaguar — 1 killed, 2 wounded

Decorations

British

Navy	VC (posthumous)	Lt-Cdr E. Esmonde
	CB	Captain C. T. M. Pizey
	DSO	Sub-Lts B. Rose, E. Lee,
		C. Kingsmill, R. M. Samples,
		Lt-Cdr R. Alexander,
		W. A. Juniper, C. Coates
	Bar to DSO	Captain J. P. Wright
	CGM	Ldg Airman D. A. Bunce
RAF	DSO	Sq-Leader W. Cliff
	DFC	Pilot Officer P. H. Carson,
		Archer and Flight-Lieut. Pett

German

Knight's Cross	Vice-Admiral Ciliax,
	Captain Hoffmann

Bibliography

Busch, Fritz Otto	*The Drama of the Scharnhorst*	London, 1956
Busch, Fritz Otto	*The Story of the Prinz Eugen*	London, 1950
Cameron, Ian	*Wings of the Morning*	London, 1962
Kemp, P. K.	*Fleet Air Arm*	London, 1954
Kemp, P. K.	*Victory at Sea*	London, 1957
Lohman, Walther, and Hildebrand, Hans	*Die Deutsche Kriegsmarine*	Bad Nauheim, 1956
Potter, John Deane	*Fiasco*	London, 1970
Robertson, Terence	*Channel Dash*	London, 1958
Roskill, Capt Stephen	*The War at Sea,* Vol II	London, 1956
Scott, Peter	*The Battle of the Narrow Seas*	London, 1946
Vulliez, Albert, and Mordal, Jacques	*Battleship Scharnhorst*	London, 1958
Command 6775/1946	*Report on the Escape of the Scharnhorst, Gneisenau and Prinz Eugen from Brest to Germany* (the Bucknill Report)	

RUSI Journal,
May 1952

*The Escape of the Scharnhorst,
Gneisenau and Prinz
Eugen.* By Wing-
Comdr J. D. Warne

Index